MEMORIALS OF THE
SPANISH
CIVIL WAR

Medal issued by the Spanish Republican Government to all members who fought in the International Brigades.

MEMORIALS OF THE
SPANISH
CIVIL WAR

The Official Publication of the International Brigade Association

Colin Williams Bill Alexander John Gorman
Foreword by Michael Foot
Introduction by Paul Preston

ALAN SUTTON PUBLISHING LIMITED

First published in the United Kingdom in 1996
Alan Sutton Publishing Ltd · Phoenix Mill · Far Thrupp
Stroud · Gloucestershire

British Library Cataloguing in Publication Data

A catalogue record for this book is available from the British Library.

ISBN 0-7509-1186-7

Book designed by Philip Gell.
Typeset in 11/13 Joanna.
Typesetting and origination by
Alan Sutton Publishing Limited.
Printed and bound in Great Britain by
Butler & Tanner, Frome, Somerset.

To the Honour and Memory of all who served in Spain
in defence of Liberty 1936–1939.

Bill Alexander

These are the arms of those who touched a sky
From which no time shall darken out their sun;
And quicken, with the blood of those who died,
These living hands for battles yet unwon.

Here speaks, at last, Jarama of their knowing
All freedoms ebbed where Ebro held its line;
Till 'Hold Madrid' rang out upon their going,
'No Spanish orphan dies, who is not mine!'

These do not die, who were in love with living,
Enough to lose it for some others' pain;
Who have the world, but did not count the giving.
Its unforgotten images of Spain.

We grasp these hands no tyrant can ignore,
Of quiet men of peace when roused to war!

Ralph Windle
South Bank 1985

John Fordham's memorial sculpture which stands in Oldham Museum.

Contents

Foreword

Michael Foot

A few years ago I stood in the office in Madrid of Felipe Gonzalez, the Prime Minister of democratic Spain, and one who has done as much as any other leader to restore and sustain democratic institutions in his country so long cursed by the Franco dictatorship. I looked across the few hundred yards of land and river which divided his office once occupied by a previous democratically elected prime minister of Spain, and the Fascist forces of the rebel Franco which after their revolt in the summer of 1936 against the Madrid government swept so close to total victory – and then, most amazingly, was halted in its tracks, across the river, for nearly three years until Republican Spain was defeated elsewhere.

Even in this century of two world wars, those three years in which democratic Madrid held its own and indeed came so near to victory were among the most critical, heroic and shameful of any recorded, although many observers or participants have had a special sinister interest in concealing or distorting the records. The crisis was a crisis for Europe and the world. If Fascism had been defeated on those Spanish battlefields, it would never have been able to launch its assaults on Britain, France, the Soviet Union and the United States of America.

The heroes were the ones who did the fighting on the spot. Most of them were Spaniards who had voted for the establishment of the Republican government in Madrid a few years before, but at critical moments they received essential aid from sympathizers abroad, either in the form of military material or, more directly, from men who came to fight and who formed an international brigade. When they appeared on several battlefields or when they marched through the streets of Madrid, they represented something more than the direct military assistance which they were offered. They represented what might be called 'the conscience of Europe': the idea that Europe was too civilized a place to tolerate the triumph of Fascist barbarism.

If the men and women who backed the cause of the Spanish Republic also had a strong strand of common sense on their side, the government which used its strength and wits to thwart their efforts deserves a special shame. All the overwhelming evidence which supported the case of the Spanish Republic was available to them. But they used their influence to suppress it.

Here is what *Tribune* wrote on 1 April 1938, one year after Franco had started his revolt and when his success was so limited that a full victory for the Republic could still have been secured. No one can say that they were not warned:

> During the past week in Rome, the Italian Fascist Party has announced that Italian troops were an essential factor in General Franco's recent victories and that they would establish a new civilisation in Mussolini's name along the western shores of the Mediterranean.

Three days ago, the Spanish rebel chiefs, no doubt to gratify the vanity of their master, published a detailed report of the part played by Italian legionaries since 9 March in the rebel offensive on the Aragon front. At the same time every responsible correspondent in Spain, including the representative of *The Times*, gave details of the role of the newly arrived Italian forces aiding Franco. Coincidentally, spokesmen of the British Government announced that they could not 'vouch for the accuracy' of statements regarding the arrival of new German and Italian forces in Spain, that 'no information' had been received by the Non-Intervention Committee which hasn't even met since 13 February.

Chamberlain himself announced that he placed 'full reliance on the intention of the Italian Government to make good their assurance' on the withdrawal of troops from Spain. In short, Chamberlain denies in London facts which Mussolini openly proclaims in Rome, whilst his experts can provide the House of Commons with no information on matters which are common gossip in Salamanca.

Yet this is the man who controls the affairs of this country during the gravest crisis in modern history. If he and his Government are allowed to continue in power, the people of Europe will be handed over to the Fascist barbarians. He will reduce Britain to a cypher in world politics. And when working class liberties have been suppressed in the remaining non-dictator countries, when the Fascists have used Chamberlain for all that he is worth as a tool and accomplice, war will come and the great cities of Britain will suffer a similar fate to Guernica, Barcelona, Bilbao, Vienna.

If the Great Powers, so-called – the international community – had shown even a small part of the combined courage and wisdom of the International Brigade, the victory of the Second World War should have been won on Spanish soil.

Michael Foot
January 1996

Preface

Their Fight for Freedom Remembered!

Swindon Memorial

All over the British Isles, in England, Scotland, Wales and Ireland, there are fifty-five memorials dedicated to the men and women who left their homes in 1936–9 to help the Spanish people defend their liberty against fascism. Sixty years after the anti-fascist war in Spain it is important to chronicle all these tributes to the Volunteers for Liberty.

In April 1939 the Swindon Branch and District Committee of the Amalgamated Engineering Union decided to erect a memorial honouring their young member, Percy Williams, who had been killed in Spain a few months before. It was the spark igniting the wish to remember all other local International Brigaders. More memorials were being planned at the time of writing.

In form, character and location they range from a simple plaque on a bench honouring Ralph Fox in the centre of Halifax to major sculptures as on the Clyde river bank in Glasgow and in Jubilee Gardens on London's South Bank. They have been placed in trade union premises, city, town and village halls, in parks and other public places. They have been erected and paid for through campaigning and support by popular and democratic organizations. They honour the action of those who volunteered to fight fascism, some of whom lost their lives and now rest in the soil of Spain. All proclaim the need to continue the fight against fascism and safeguard liberty today. Around 2,400 men and women went to Spain from Britain. Five hundred and twenty-six were never to return to their homes – they were killed.

Why is it, after so many years and so many wars, that all these memorials have been erected to the volunteers of the International Brigade?

The International Brigades have inspired many books, plays, music and films. The memorials are lasting forms of this interest. They show that men and women are prepared to face risks and even death for their ideals. They demonstrate that people from different countries and races can cooperate, work and fight together. They show that people have resources and abilities which can be released and harnessed in common struggle. The existence of the memorials recalls the deep roots of democratic and international solidarity. They convey confidence that lasting liberty and peace for all can be won.

The period of the thirties was a time of concern and questioning, especially among younger people, about the future for jobs, freedom and peace. Poverty and unemployment were affecting the traditional centres of industry. There was anger and alarm at the attacks on the working people, minority groups and their organizations when fascism triumphed in Italy, Germany and Austria. The growth in Britain of the activity and influence of fascist organizations and ideas heightened these fears. The hopes for peace were undermined by emergent militarism in Hitler's Germany and Italian aggression in Abyssinia. Some newspapers, politicians and academics claimed that fascism was invincible and inevitable. It was a stage in the development of human society and nothing could be done about it. These ideas were rejected and opposed by only small groups at first.

Cargo vessel taking supplies to the Republican forces hit by Italian bombers off the coast of Spain.

The character and fight against fascism moved centre stage when, in 1936, Franco attempted to overthrow by force the Popular Front Government of Republican Spain. In Britain at the time there was little knowledge of Spain, its people, life and politics. The brutal repression of the striking Asturian miners in 1934 by the army commanded by Franco aroused anger and solidarity here, especially in the mining communities. The rebellion of the generals, the big landowners and industrialists heightened concern and questioning about Spanish affairs. Would fascism be able to score yet another victory? Would there be destruction of the popular, democratic forces? Would all the dictatorships gain more influence and strength? Spain was no longer a remote far-away country. It was seen as the setting and focus of struggle against fascism and reaction. The news of the open military help to Franco from Hitler and Mussolini, and the heroic resistance of the people of Madrid, Barcelona and the big cities fired a widespread wish to help the Republic and its people.

An Aid Spain movement developed in many towns, cities, coalfields and factories which drew in wide groupings of people. Many thousands contributed and helped to collect food, medical supplies and money for the Spanish people who were short of everything. There was political activity stretching across party lines, trying to change the Conservative Government help for Franco by ending the Non-Intervention Agreement which prevented the Popular Front Government buying arms for its defence. Pressure was exerted on those in the Labour Party and trade unions who supported Non-Intervention.

Others wished to join and help the Spanish fighters in their armed struggle. In the first days of the fascist rebellion a few individuals from

The Cockney Express arrives in Spain from England with food for Madrid.

Spanish militia showing their defiance during the early days of the war. Note the solitary female (front, third left) and the trade union initials UGT on the cap of a militiaman (first right).

Britain travelled to Spain and joined up with the people's militia groups. As the number of volunteers from all over the world increased they were organized and welcomed by the Republican Government. They became the International Brigade in the Republican Army.

Around 2,400 volunteered from the British Isles and the then British Empire. There can be no exact figure because the Conservative Government, in its support for the Non-Intervention Agreement, threatened to use the Foreign Enlistment Act of 1875 which they declared made volunteering illegal. Keeping records and lists of names was dangerous and difficult. However, no-passport weekend trips to Paris provided a way round for all who left these shores en route for Spain. In France active support from French people opened the paths over the Pyrenees.

The British volunteers came from all walks of life, all parts of the British Isles and the then British Empire. The great majority were from the industrial areas, especially those of heavy industry. They were accustomed to the discipline associated with working in factories and pits. They learnt from the organization, democracy and solidarity of trade unionism.

Despite the setback suffered by the unions as a result of the 1926 General Strike, many volunteers continued to display loyalty to their unions and held positions of trust and responsibilty in them. Nearly all trades and professions were represented among the volunteers, the most numerous being miners and dockers.

Many had experienced unemployment or were unemployed when they volunteered and consequently were bitter and deeply critical of the society which condemned them to poverty. They became involved in the activities of the National Unemployed Workers' Movement, taking part in meetings, marches and protests of all kinds.

The Hunger Marches to London and the local Means Test offices provided rich lessons in organization and solidarity and the need to integrate individual ideas and opinions in service of the overall cause. From their ranks sprang leaders in Spain, like Peter Kerrigan, Bill Paynter and Harry Dobson.

Intellectuals, academics, writers and poets were an important force in the early groups of volunteers. They had the means to get to Spain and were accustomed to travelling, whereas very few workers had left British shores. They went because of their growing alienation from a society that had failed miserably to meet the needs of so many people and because of their deep repugnance at the burning of books in Nazi Germany, the persecution of individuals, the glorification of war and the whole philosophy of fascism.

Military identity book which every International Brigader carried.

Among the volunteers were men who had served in the armed forces. Enlistment in the army or navy meant regular meals, money to keep their families at a time of mass unemployment and grinding poverty. Experience in the forces and their repressive role in the colonies helped to mould political outlooks and the struggle in Spain was viewed as the logical next step to change society and social conditions.

They came from all political parties and from none. They were united around one common ideology, opposition to fascism. This unity was emphasized in the Republican Army Pay Book where under the heading 'Political Affiliation' all wrote 'Anti-fascista'.

The International Brigades and the British volunteers were, numerically, only a small part of the Republican forces, but nearly all had accepted the need for organization and order in civilian life. Many already knew how to lead in the trade unions, demonstrations and people's organizations, the need to set an example and lead from the front if necessary. They were united in their aims and prepared to fight for them. The International Brigades provided a shock force while the Republic trained and organized an army from an assemblage of individuals. The Spanish people knew they were not fighting alone.

The International Brigades learned from their struggles that courage and conviction were important, but could not prevail against the vast weapon

Woodcut of the International Brigade badge.

superiority which rested in the open military intervention by the dictators and the British obstruction of Republican arms purchase.

The volunteers realized that popular pressure in Britain could and had to end the policies of Non-Intervention. Fighting at the front they wrote home to families, friends, work places, trade unions and political organizations to oppose the Tories and supporters of Non-Intervention. Their letters were widely read and often published in local newspapers. Wounded Brigaders were often sent home to recuperate and relate their experiences – always demanding 'Arms for Spain'. This activity lifted the Aid Spain campaign, deepened the anti-fascist feelings and increased the opposition to Prime Minister Chamberlain's appeasement policies. The ties between the Brigaders and their communities grew and were cemented.

Prime Minister Negrin's decision in September 1938 to send all Brigaders out of Spain was met with mixed feelings. There was some relief at escaping from hardship and danger, but all knew the Spanish people had been left to fight on against the dictators' onslaught. The survivors back in Britain received a popular, emotional welcome as anti-fascist fighters. Sam Wild, last Commander of the British Battalion, pledged to continue the fight in Britain to help the Spanish regain democracy. The returned Brigaders formed an association in March 1939 with the aim of winning all necessary support for the Spanish Republic. They gave an uplift and reinforcement for the Aid Spain movement. Renewed efforts were made to compel the Tory Government to end its support for the dictators. But it was in vain. Franco fascism achieved military victory on 30 March 1939. The Spanish people were victims of a 35-year-long period of executions, prison and repression.

Five months after Franco's victory, the world war which the Brigaders had tried to avert, began. The aim 'Save Spain, Save Peace' had not been achieved. Brigaders realized that only the defeat of the major fascist powers – Germany and Italy – could open a path for the Spanish people to regain their own freedom. Facing some discrimination they took their places in the armed forces, the civil defence services and the war effort.

Despite all the problems of wartime Britain, the suffering of the Spanish people under Franco was not forgotten. Money and material aid were collected and, overcoming difficulties, were taken to the Spanish opposition and to International Brigaders interned in camps. Contacts were made with Republicans and Brigaders who were in the resistance movements in fascist-occupied Europe. When Hitler's bombs fell on London and Coventry the people recalled with bitterness La Pasionaria's warning: 'Stop the bombs on Madrid and Barcelona today or they may fall on London and Paris tomorrow.' It was a warning ignored by the Tories.

With the military defeat of Hitler and Mussolini in 1945 there was widespread hope that Franco would be removed and so complete the defeat of the fascist powers. It did not happen. For another thirty years Franco's dictatorial regime repressed the people.

Campaigning in Britain for solidarity with the Spanish people's struggle against fascism in which twenty-two International Brigaders took part. The photograph shows the two drivers (with peaked caps), Clive Branson, Mary Slater, Alan Gilchrist, Arthur Nicoll and Joe Fuhr (respectively second, sixth, seventh, eighth and ninth from the left).

Right: Spanish Medical Aid ambulance about to go out to Spain.

Emblem of the International Brigade presented to all volunteers by the Republican Government in 1938.

Bill Alexander, probably in January / February 1938 in Teruel.

In Britain there was a broad continuing campaign exposing and condemning his rule. Marches and demonstrations, meetings and conferences demanded an end to any recognition and support for the Franco regime. Funds were collected and smuggled into Spain for the families of prisoners condemned for demanding human rights. MPs of all parties and legal personalities were sent to observe and report on the trials in military courts of those who dared opposed the dictatorship. The Spanish people were never forgotten. Franco never overcame the popular detestation of his regime.

After Franco's death attempts to continue a dictatorial regime failed, a factor for this being the wish of the Spanish people for democracy. That had been kept alive by the continuing opposition inside Spain, helped by popular support in Britain and Europe.

The defeat of the attempts to continue with fascism, the formation of open political parties, both left and right, the right of free association in trade unions, elections at all levels and an open press showed the strength of the forces determined to build a democratic society. It showed that the Spanish people's organizations were strong enough to decide on their own steps, their own forms of democracy and freedom.

The International Brigade Association had made a contribution to bring this about. It had strong emotional ties with the Spanish people and faced with the emergence of fascism and racism it could explain the lessons of unity and struggle gained from the past. It is recognized that Volunteers for Liberty were far-seeing and right to go to fight fascism.

The story of these fifty-five memorials to the International Brigaders is a permanent reminder of the anti-fascist struggle in Spain.

Freedom was never held without a fight.
Without struggle there can be no victory.

Bill Alexander

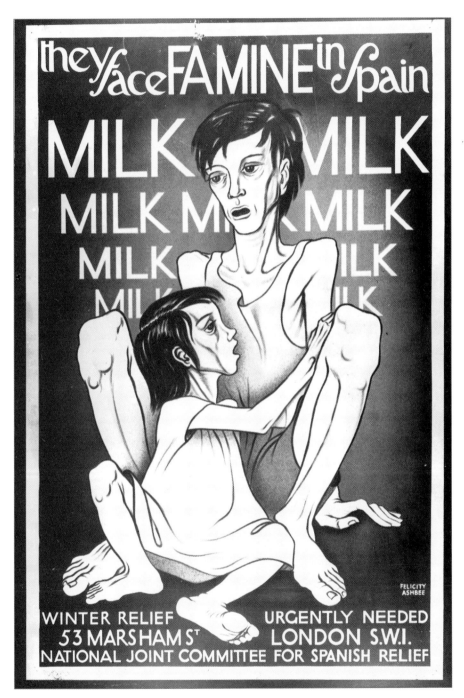

Thirties poster by Felicity Ashbee.

Acknowledgements

This book has been made possible by the generous financial support of the Lipman Trust, the Barry Amiel and Norman Melburn Trust and many trades unions at national and local level.

We are indebted to all members of the International Brigade Association who have kept up activities over long years, inspiring and helping the creation of the memorials.

Information has been made available by: the Marx Memorial Library from the International Brigade Archive, the Museum of Working Class History in Manchester, the Miners' Library in Swansea and the Irish Labour Movement Museum in Dublin.

We are grateful to the local authorities that have sponsored, created the memorials and provided photographs and information: Aberdare, Aberdeen, Birmingham, Blyth Valley, Bristol, Camden, Cardiff, Cunninghame, Dundee, Edinburgh, Glasgow, Greater London, Halifax, Hull, Kirkcaldy, Leeds, Liverpool, Manchester, Middlesbrough, Newcastle upon Tyne, Nottinghamshire, Oldham, Penygroes, Prestonpans, Rhondda, Rotherham, Sheffield, Southwark, St Helens, Stoke-on-Trent, Strathclyde and Thameside.

We thank those trade union and other bodies that have initiated and arranged memorials: Aberdeen Trades Council, Dublin Trade Union Council; Leicester Socialist Centre; Manufacturing Science Finance Union West of England region, St Lukes Church, Peckham, Society of Graphical and Allied Trades, Swindon Amalgamated Engineering Union, Transport and General Workers' Union, Tyne and Wear Trades Council, the University of Kent, Waterford (Republic of Ireland) and the Amalgamated Transport and General Workers Union.

The authors would like to express their deep appreciation and thanks to the many, many people who have enthusiastically committed energy, time and help of all kinds in campaigning for the memorials and in the preparation of this book.

All historical photographs, unless otherwise stated, are from the International Brigade Association archive in the Marx Memorial Library.

Photograph and Illustration Credits

Famine poster: *John Gorman*
Jubilee Gardens memorial and group around it: *Ian Walters*
Bill Alexander at IBA Archive: *Nigel Tanburn*
Jack Jones and memorial: *P.J. Arkell*
Unity Theatre and cover of memorial progamme: *Unity Theatre Archive*
Patience Edney and Wally Togwell: *Nigel Tanburn*
Camden memorial plaque: *Nigel Tanburn*
Southwark Mayor with Osipenko: *Southwark Borough Council*
Southwark memorial plaque: *Southwark Borough Council*
Revd Andrew Davey and the Red Stole: *Nigel Tanburn*
Plaque in Aberdeen Concert Hall: *Aberdeen Council*
Veterans in 15th Brigade Library: *Aberdeen Unemployment Centre*
John Londragan plaque: *Aberdeen Unemployment Centre*
Glasgow memorial and Baillieston Library: *Glasgow City Council*
Veterans at Edinburgh East Princes Street Gardens: *Douglas Robertson*
Dundee Peace Gardens memorial: *Dundee Council*
John Smith memorial plaque: *Cunninghame District Council*
Cardiff memorial: *Cardiff City Council*
Welsh national memorial plaque: postcard, issued by *Swansea Miners' Library*
Swansea Miners' Library, Hendrefoilan House: *Larry Childness*
Aberdare memorial plaque: *John Wright*
Rhondda memorial plaque: *Newman*
George Fretwell: property of his brother *Dafydd Fretwell*
Plaque to George Fretwell: *J. Wright*
Frank Graham at the memorial tree and plaques: *R. Rowley*
Newcastle City Council plaque: *Newcastle City Council*
View of Bob Elliot House and residents: *Blyth Valley District Council*
Middlesbrough memorial plaque: *Middlesbrough Council*
Manchester memorial plaque: *Martin Jenkinson*
Oldham memorial: *Martin Jenkinson*
Bernard McCormick and memorial: *St Helens Town Council*
Memorial seat and stone obelisk to Tommy James in Rotherham Peace Garden:
   David Groucher
Leeds memorial plaque: *Leeds City Council*
Carved stone memorial: *Sheffield City Council*
Ceramic memorial: *Stoke City Council*
Part of Nottinghamshire memorial: *Michael Johnson*
Birmingham Peace Garden: *Jim Saunders*
Memorial plaque: *Jim Saunders*
Leicester memorial: *Alternative Services Cooperative*
Group around memorial bench: *University of Kent at Canterbury*
Swindon memorial headstone: *Len Thompson*
British Battalion banner: *Nigel Tanburn*
Banner presented by the women of Barcelona: *Nigel Tanburn*

Introduction

The International Brigades in the Spanish Civil War

The years from 1918 to 1939 were an era of virtually uninterrupted rightist assault on the organized working class. The crushing of revolution in Germany and Hungary after the First World War was followed by the destruction of the Italian left by Mussolini, the establishment of dictatorships in Spain and Portugal and the defeat of the General Strike in Britain. The rise of Hitler saw the annihilation of the most powerful working-class movement in Western Europe and in 1934 the Austrian left was smashed by Dollfuss. Austria stands out because there, for the first time, workers took up arms against fascism in 1934. Tragically, it was too late and the domino effect continued in country after country in central Europe.

The Spanish Civil War, which broke out in July 1936, was to be the fiercest battle in a European civil war which had been under way since the Bolshevik triumph of 1917. The Spanish war was essentially Spanish in origin. In the first two years of the Second Republic in Spain, between 1931 and 1933, a

'Forward!'

coalition of moderate socialists and middle-class liberal Republicans had attempted to carry through a programme of social reform, especially in the countryside. The success of right-wing resistance impelled the socialists to fight the November 1933 elections alone in the hope of establishing an exclusively socialist government. In a system which favoured coalitions, this handed victory to a rightist coalition. Throughout 1934, that coalition overturned the minimal social and religious reforms of 1931–3. Fearful that the right planned to establish a fascist state, socialists, anarchists and communists rose up in the mining districts of Asturias only to be defeated by the Army under the supervision of General Francisco Franco. It was the first battle of the Civil War. The right took its revenge in a savage repression which impelled the left to reunite in the Popular Front. In the February 1936 elections, the Popular Front won a narrow victory and immediately began to revive the reforming programme of 1931.

Alarmed by the confidence of the left, the right prepared for war. A military conspiracy was led by General Emilio Mola. The growing fascist party, Falange Española, used terror squads to create the disorder to justify the imposition of an authoritarian regime. The left's response contributed to the spiral of violence. The plotters rose on 18 July not expecting a long war. The rising succeeded in the provincial capitals of conservative Catholic Castile, but was defeated by the workers in Madrid, Barcelona and the major industrial cities of the north. However, once the rebels' strongest card, the brutal colonial Army of Africa, under General Franco, had crossed the Straits of Gibraltar in transport aircraft supplied by Hitler and Mussolini, the over-optimistic coup was converted into a long and bloody civil war.

The assistance given to Franco by Hitler and Mussolini was not disinterested, for they knew that, in giving it, they were also undermining the position of the Western powers who covertly applauded the destruction of a Republic they assumed to be a Soviet puppet. It was hardly surprising that the activities of foreign powers would dictate both the course and outcome of the Spanish Civil War. Much of the energy of the right in Europe during the interwar period was devoted to trying both internationally and domestically to build barriers against real and perceived revolutionary threats. Fear and suspicion of the Soviet Union had been a major determinant of the diplomacy of the Western powers throughout the 1920s. In the context of world depression and increased working-class militancy, anti-bolshevism became even more decisive in the 1930s. The relative tolerance shown initially by Britain and the United States to both Hitler and Mussolini implied a tacit approval of fascist policies towards the left in general and towards communism in particular.

Accordingly, the war between the Spanish left and right had wide international ramifications. The Spanish Popular Front Government turned immediately for help to its French counterpart. Out of fascist solidarity and out of a desire to weaken France, the German and Italian dictators agreed to send aircraft without which the Spanish rebels would not have been able to transport their best troops for use on the Spanish mainland. Similarly, Soviet arms would play a crucial part in the defence of Madrid not just so much out of ideological solidarity, but because Stalin did not want to see the French counterweight to Germany weakened.

For Italian, German and Austrian refugees from fascism and nazism, however, the Spanish Civil War was the first real chance to fight back and eventually to go home. Volunteers from the democracies made the hazardous

City of the Dead – Guernica, devastated by Nazi bombers in the first ever mass aerial bombing of a town.

A battlefield in Spain, probably Brunete, showing Soviet tanks on the move.

journey to Spain out of anxiety about what defeat for the Spanish Republic
might mean for the rest of the world. The volunteers overcame enormous
difficulties to fight for the Republic. Some were out of work, others were
intellectuals, a few adventurers, but all had come to fight fascism. The
International Brigades, dubbed by the poet Louis McNeice 'a rag-tag army' of
volunteers, were organized under the auspices of the Comintern in the late
summer and early autumn of 1936, although it is clear that the communists
were merely providing the channels for a widespread spontaneous movement.

Volunteers from all over the world arrived in Spain via Paris in October
and were trained at Albacete. The first units reached Madrid on
8 November, and consisted of German and Italian anti-fascists, plus some
British, French and Polish left-wingers. Some of them had either fought in
the First World War or else had some experience of military service.
Accordingly, they were able to pass on much basic military know-how to
the Spanish militiamen with whom they fought. Sprinkled among the
Spanish defenders at the rate of one to four, the Brigaders both boosted
their morale and trained them in the use of machine-guns, in the
conservation of ammunition, and how to use cover.

Recruitment was largely organized by the Communist Parties. Not all
volunteers were communists, although many were. Political affiliation did
not affect the idealism and heroism of those who sacrificed their comfort,
their security and often their lives in the anti-fascist struggle. It was,
nevertheless, the communists who smuggled the volunteers across the
French border, either on foot or in buses. Some even crossed the Pyrenees
wearing rope-soled sandals or alpargatas.

After their crucial role in the defence of Madrid against the initial rebel
assault, in December and January the International Brigades played a decisive
part in fighting off the various efforts made by the Nationalists to cut the
Madrid–La Coruña road to the north-west. Casualties among the
International Brigades were particularly high. This was hardly surprising
given the disparity in training and equipment enjoyed by Franco's hardened
colonial army. After the fall of Malaga in February, the rebels launched a
huge attack through the Jarama valley on the Madrid–Valencia highway to
the east of the capital. This was defended fiercely by Republican troops
reinforced by the International Brigades. In the view of Hemingway, the
attack was 'stupidly conceived and executed'. The Nationalist front advanced
a few miles, but made no strategic gain. The Republicans lost 25,000
including some of the best British and American members of the Brigades,
and the Nationalists 20,000. The International Brigades bore the brunt of
the fighting. The British contingent was almost wiped out in one afternoon.

In March the Nationalists made further efforts to encircle Madrid by
attacking Guadalajara, forty miles north-east of Madrid. An army of
50,000, the best-equipped and most heavily armed force yet seen in the
war, broke through, but were defeated by a Republican counter-attack
involving the Garibaldi Battalion of the International Brigade. Thereafter,

as the Republic progressed in the organization of its Ejército Popular (People's Army), and as the conflict turned into a more conventional war of large-scale manoeuvre, the Brigades played an important but less central role. After each engagement, there were fewer survivors. Yet after each engagement, they went willingly back into battle. Poorly clad, shod and equipped, they fought on, held together by shared ideals rather than conventional structures of hierarchy and discipline.

The Brigades played a substantial role in later offensives – the capture of Belchite and Teruel and in the final defensive phase of the war following Franco's great offensive through the spring and summer of 1938. This followed on from the defeat of the great Republican attack against Teruel, which briefly held the town from 8 January to 21 February 1938. Within two weeks, the Nationalists launched a gigantic offensive through Aragon and Castellon towards the sea. A hundred thousand troops, well covered by 200 tanks and nearly 1,000 German and Italian aircraft, began their advance on 7 March 1938. By 15 April they had reached the Mediterranean. In July, Franco launched a major attack on Valencia. The Republican forces, including the International Brigades, demonstrated heroic determination in defence and delayed the inexorable Nationalist advance. In late July 1938, to relieve the threat against Valencia, the Republic mounted a spectacular diversion in the form of an attempt to restore contact with Catalonia, an assault across the River Ebro. In the most

15th Brigade Anti-Tank Battery commander Arthur Nicoll (second right) and (left to right) gun commanders Chris Smith, Mino Saturnino, Jimmy Sullivan and Otto Esterson.

Off to the front again after convalescence.

hard-fought battle of the entire war, the Republican army of 80,000 men crossed the river and broke through the Nationalist lines, although at great cost to the International Brigade. By 1 August they had reached Gandesa, Francoist reinforcements were rushed in and the Republicans were subjected to three months of fierce artillery bombardment and sweltering heat. Determined to smash the Republican army, Franco gathered over 30,000 fresh troops with new German equipment. By mid-November, at horrendous cost in casualties, the Francoists had pushed the Republicans out of the territory captured in July.

In the hope of changing the attitude of the Western powers, the Republican Government decided unilaterally to withdraw its foreign volunteers. A farewell parade was held in Barcelona for the International Brigades on 29 October 1938. Before thousands of tearful, but cheering, Spaniards, the communist leader Dolores Ibarruri, La Pasionaria, made an intensely moving speech:

> Comrades of the International Brigades! Political reasons, reasons of state, the good of that same cause for which you offered your blood with limitless generosity, send some of you back to your countries and some to forced exile. You can go with pride. You are history. You are legend. You are the heroic example of the solidarity and universality of democracy. . . . We shall not forget you; and when the olive tree of peace puts forth its leaves, entwined with the laurels of the Spanish Republic's victory, come back! Come back to us and here you will find a homeland.

It is difficult to calculate exactly the total number of volunteers. Figures vary from a minimum of 40,000 to a maximum of 60,000 from fifty different countries going to fight against fascism in Spain. Nearly 20 per cent of them died and most suffered wounds of varying degrees of severity. In October 1938 more than 12,000 were still in Spain. They began the slow journey home or back into exile, often to fates more appalling than anything they had yet suffered. Those who survived were not to return to Spain until after the death of Franco thirty-seven years later.

It is impossible to evaluate with certainty the impact of the International Brigades. On innumerable occasions, at the siege of Madrid, the battles of Jarama, Guadalajara and Brunete, they contributed decisively to Republican survival. Some have argued that a Republican victory would have permitted Hitler's troops to have rolled on to Gibraltar after the defeat of France. But that is the worst kind of counter-factual history. Franco believed, rightly, that he had done Hitler an enormous service in defeating the Republic because of the way in which he had both exposed the weakness of appeasement and specifically altered the balance of power against the Western allies both internationally and also in terms of internal French politics. The Republican victory for which the Brigaders fought might very well have stiffened French resistance, might have avoided the Hitler–Stalin pact, severely dented Mussolini's confidence, withal possibly even have avoided the Second World War altogether. However, that is mere speculation. What is certain is that the Spanish Republic severely weakened the military capacity of fascist Italy. Moreover, as long as the Republic fought on, Hitler was unlikely to attack France and therefore the British had longer to rearm.

In moral terms, the value of the Brigades as a beacon of anti-fascism was incalculable. On 22 June 1937, shortly before his death in battle, an American volunteer named Gene Wolman wrote to his family:

> For the first time in history, for the first time since Fascism began systematically throttling and rending all we hold dear, we are getting the opportunity to fight back. Mussolini rode unopposed . . . to Rome. Hitler boasts that he took power without bloodshed . . . In little Asturias the miners made a brave, but unsuccessful stand against the combined reactionaries of Spain. In Ethiopia the Fascist machine was again able to work its will without any unified opposition. Even in Democratic America the majority have had to undergo every sort of oppression without being able to fight back . . . Here finally the oppressed of the Earth are united, here finally we have weapons, here we can fight back. Here, even if we lose . . . in the fight itself, in the weakening of Fascism, we will have won.

November 1938 in Marsa, Catalonia, one of the farewell parades before the International Brigades were sent home.

Paul Preston
Professor of Contemporary Spanish History at the London School of Economics

The Memorials

Location of Memorials

Jubilee Gardens, South Bank, London

IBA Archive, Marx Memorial Library, 37a Clerkenwell Green, London

TGWU, Transport House, 16 Palace Street, London

Unity Theatre destroyed by fire – former site Goldington Street, St Pancras, London

Camden Town Hall, Euston Road, London

Southwark memorial, Mayor's Parlour, Town Hall, Peckham Road, London

St Luke's Church, Farnborough Way, North Peckham, London

Concert Hall, Aberdeen

Trades Council Club, Aberdeen

15th Brigade Library, Aberdeen Unemployment Centre, 54 Frederick Street, Aberdeen

Aberdeen Trades Council Headquarters, John Londragan House

Clyde River Bank, Custom House Quay, Glasgow

Public Library, Baillieston, Glasgow

East Princes Street Gardens, Edinburgh

Forth Avenue, Kirkcaldy, Fife

Peace Gardens outside MacManus Galleries, Albert Square, Dundee

Civic Square, Prestonpans, Lothian

Seat in local park, Prestonpans, Lothian
Cunninghame House Branch Library, Friars Cross, Irvine
Dooega, Achill Island, Co. Mayo, Ireland
Liberty Hall, Eden Quay, Dublin
Morley's Bridge, Kilgarvan, Co. Kerry, Ireland
ATGWU Hall, Keyser Street, Waterford, Ireland
Alexandra Gardens, Cathays Park, Cardiff
Miners' Library, Hendrefoilan House, Gower Road, Swansea
Central Library, Aberdare
Rhondda Council Chamber, Pentre, Rhondda
Village Hall, Penygroes, Gwynedd
Grounds of City Hall, Newcastle upon Tyne
Bob Elliot House, Wright Street, Blyth, Northumberland
Town Hall, Middlesbrough
Resource Centre, Hardman Street, Liverpool
Town Hall, Albert Square, Manchester
Borough Museum, City Hall, Oldham
Town Hall, Corporation Street, St Helens
Unemployed Resource Centre in College Street, St Helens,
    which no longer functions
Bull Green, Halifax
Peace Garden, corner of Wharncliffe Street and Doncaster Road,
    Rotherham
Foyer, City Hall, George Street, Leeds
Peace Garden, outside City Hall, Sheffield
Guild Hall, Alfred Gelder Street, Hull
Town Hall, Glebe Street, Stoke-on-Trent
County Hall, West Bridgeford, Nottingham
St Thomas Peace Garden, Bath Row, Birmingham
Peace Walk, Victoria Park, University Road, Leicester
Green in front of Civic Centre, Castle Street, Reading
Rutherford College, University of Kent, Canterbury
Castle Park, Bristol
MSF Office, 1 Tenbury Road, Westbury-on-Trym, Bristol
Whitworth Road Cemetery, Swindon
Coate Water Park, Swindon
SOGAT Convalescent Home, Rottingdean, Sussex

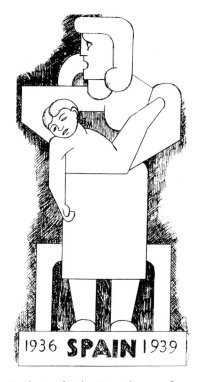

Line drawing of Reading Memorial on cover of programme for the unveiling ceremony.

Jubilee Gardens, South Bank, London

London

Barcelona, Saturday 29 October 1938. Many, many thousands throng the main street, mostly women and children who with tears of gratitude and flowers embrace International Brigaders parading before Republican President Manuel Azana and Prime Minister Juan Negrin and other political and military leaders to bid farewell. The voice of the beloved Spanish leader Dolores Ibarruri, La Pasionaria, fills the air with the pledge:

> We shall not forget you; and when the olive tree of peace puts forth its leaves, entwined with the laurels of the Spanish Republic's victory, come back!

London, Jubilee Gardens, Saturday 5 October 1985. The distance between Barcelona 1938 and London 1985 is not measured in time alone, but also by the sacrifice of millions to vanquish the forces of dictatorship and fascism the world over so that liberty could flourish and the olive tree of peace put forth its leaves again in Spain.

On that day they gathered before the historic International Brigade banner made and presented by the women of Barcelona to the British Battalion at that farewell parade. They came, these veterans of the International Brigade, with their memories to Jubilee Gardens, assembled together as they were forty-seven years earlier in Barcelona, to salute their brothers and sisters, comrades in arms who fell on Spanish soil fighting to defend democracy and warn the world.

They came from the four corners of Britain, from Ireland, France, Bulgaria and the German Democratic Republic to participate with some 8,000 men, women and children in the unveiling of a memorial next to the old County Hall to the members of the British Battalion of the International Brigade.

The highly emotional farewell parade of the International Brigades at the Diagonal, the main street in Barcelona, when they were showered with bouquets.

4

INTERNATIONAL
BRIGADE

IN HONOUR OF OVER 2100 MEN &
WOMEN VOLUNTEERS WHO LEFT
THESE SHORES TO FIGHT SIDE
BY SIDE WITH THE SPANISH PEOPLE
IN THEIR HEROIC STRUGGLE
AGAINST FASCISM 1936 -1939
MANY WERE WOUNDED AND
MAIMED 526 WERE KILLED
THEIR EXAMPLE INSPIRED
THE WORLD

After the unveiling on 5 October 1985 (left to right) Bill Alexander, Janet Vaughan, Michael Foot, Norman Willis and Tony Banks gather by the memorial.

They were entertained by the Maerdy & Tylorstown Colliery Silver Band, South Wales, from where many volunteered for Spain and many died on its soil.

Among the speakers were Tony Banks (Chairman of the Greater London Council), Norman Willis (TUC general secretary), Janet Vaughan (who had helped organize Spanish Medical Aid), Bill Alexander (International Brigade Memorial Appeal chairman) and Michael Foot (the former leader of the Labour Party), who unveiled the monument.

This is a unique memorial; no other country has erected anything comparable to members of the International Brigades. Its erection had the backing of prominent figures in the labour and trade union movement and of professional people. It is situated opposite the Houses of Parliament on a prestigious site on the banks of the River Thames.

The memorial sculpture with its plinth stands four and a half metres high, the four powerful figures hold up a wounded kneeling form, their free arms stretch up high above their heads – two with open palms in the act of fending off to protect, and two with fists clenched, expressing defiant resistance.

One of the drawings from Felicia Browne's sketch book which appear throughout this book. Her story is told on pp. 20–21.

In a poem dedicated to the memorial the son of an International Brigader, Ralph Windle, wrote:

> These are the arms of those who touched a sky
> From which no time shall darken out their sun;
> And quicken, with the blood of those who died,
> These living hands for battles yet unwon.

There are inscriptions carved on the four faces of the plinth.

On the front: 'International Brigade. In honour of over 2,100 men and women volunteers who left these shores to fight side by side with the Spanish people in their heroic struggle against fascism, 1936–1939. Many were wounded and maimed. 526 were killed. Their example inspired the world.' The significance of the phrase 'who left these shores' is that those who went to Spain via Britain, included volunteers from Australia, Cyprus, Egypt, Hong Kong, Ireland and South Africa.

On one side, a paraphrase of lines from C. Day Lewis: 'They went because their open eyes could see no other way.'

On the second side are lines from Byron: 'Yet Freedom! yet thy banner, torn, but flying, Streams like the thunder-storm against the wind.'

On the rear: 'This memorial unveiled by Michael Foot, October 5 1985, was made possible by the support of many democratic organisations, individuals and the Greater London Council.'

The International Brigade Memorial Appeal was launched early in 1984. By the end of the year many hundreds of individuals and trade union and democratic bodies of a wide variety had contributed to it.

From a number of sculptors, five were asked to submit their ideas for the memorial. Some very fine designs resulted but eventually the maquette by Ian Walters was selected as symbolizing, in a most powerful and moving manner, the magnificent support the people of many nations gave to aid the Spanish people in their fight against fascism.

Appreciation was expressed by the Appeal Committee especially to the Greater London Council for both its significant financial support and for providing the beautiful site on the South Bank of the River Thames, where the memorial can be seen and appreciated by Londoners and by those from the rest of the country and other lands who visit the capital.

There is a pilgrimage of remembrance every year at the memorial by members and supporters of the International Brigade Association when fresh flowers are laid at the plinth.

The continued existence of the memorial is threatened today by commercial developers who care little about the preservation of open green spaces or about those who fought for liberty.

The memorial in Jubilee Gardens on the South Bank of the Thames, London.

International Brigade Memorial Archive, London

London

The good and mighty of departed ages
Are in their graves, the innocent and free,
Heroes, and Poets, and prevailing Sages,
Who leave the vesture of their majesty
To adorn and clothe this naked world . . .

Shelley

Bill Alexander looking up information in the IBA Memorial Archive catalogue with part of the archive collection behind him in Marx Memorial Library, Clerkenwell Green, London.

The House on the Green, Marx Memorial Library, in the heart of London at Clerkenwell Green, is a unique repository of the inspiring history of the 'good and mighty of departed ages' and among its treasures is the International Brigade Memorial Archive, a worthy tribute to the volunteers of the British Battalion who fought and died in the battle

against fascism in Spain and to those who survived to continue the struggle for democracy and liberty.

The Library is on a site rich in radical history and which was described in the *City Press* in 1871 as 'the headquarters of republicanism, revolution and ultra non-conformity'. It is housed in a building completed in 1738 as the Welch Charity School, which in its time has served as a public house and as the Coffee Rooms, where Marx met with his International Working Men's Association. In 1892 the Social Democratic Federation leased the building for its Twentieth Century Press (TCP) and the journal *Justice*. Several of the earliest English editions of the works of Marx and Engels were issued by the TCP. Lenin in exile produced *Iskra* the Russian Social Democratic newspaper from an office in the building.

In 1933, on the 50th anniversary of the death of Marx, the year which also saw the Nazis burning books in Germany, the Marx Memorial Library and Workers School was established at the building, 37a Clerkenwell Green. Threatened with demolition in 1963 to provide green space, a very broad successful campaign to save the building ensued and the Grade II listed building was restored finally in 1969 with the assistance of the Greater London Council and National Heritage.

The International Brigade Memorial Archive was donated by the International Brigade Association to Marx House and its contents are concentrated on the years from the outbreak of the anti-fascist war in Spain in 1936 to the death of Franco in 1975.

It is the most comprehensive collection on the subject in the UK and can only be compared to the archive of the Spanish Socialist Party, the State archive in Spain or the Moscow archive. A microfiche copy of all the contents has been made and held in the building where it can be viewed so that handling of the original material, some of which is fragile, is minimized. The contents of the archive were catalogued in three volumes by the late IBA secretary Nan Green, who served in Spain with the British medical units, and archivist A.D. Atienza. The catalogues have been deposited in university and specialist libraries both at home and abroad. This has enabled a steady stream of students, post-graduate researchers, family historians, writers and television and theatrical producers to find their way to the archive.

The archive is housed downstairs in the main lecture hall of Marx House and comprises two large cabinets containing boxes of documentary material which form the main body of the archive, a book collection (mostly in English and Spanish) in a glass-fronted cabinet which also exhibits various memorabilia, and posters and banners, also stored in the cabinets. The striking historic red banner of the British Battalion showing a clenched fist and a roll call of battles the British volunteers fought in is on view in the hall, preserved within an airtight glazed frame. The banner was made and presented by the women of Barcelona.

A quick glance at the boxes reveals a wealth of materials. Among papers of individuals there are sketches made at the front of Brigaders by the young artist Clive Branson; press cuttings from 1936 to 1966, including some from the *Morning Post*, the *Daily Telegraph* and the *Manchester Guardian* on events connected with or in Spain collected by J. Vincente Barrogan, teacher of Spanish at London University, documents on the foundation of the IBA and its development, and despatches from the front in Spain to the *Daily Worker* from Peter Kerrigan, communist and Scottish leader and one of the British commissars at the Albacete base.

The files contain verses by Miles Tomalin, probably written in May 1937. In the middle of the Brunete battle, this young writer and poet from London, fighting with the Anti-Tank Battery, wrote:

> He gives but he has all to gain,
> He watches not for Spain alone.
> Beyond him stand the homes of Spain,
> Behind him stands his own.

Miles Tomalin playing the recorder and Otto Esterson the mandolin, during a cultural break from fighting with the Anti-Tank Battery.

This particular verse, which reveals how well the volunteer understood why he was fighting in Spain, was used in a New Year greeting card for members of the 15th Brigade to send home. Miles Tomalin was responsible for a lively wall newspaper which was often attached to an olive tree or a pile of ammunition boxes.

There are hundreds of photographs in the collection, among them of: volunteers crossing the Pyrenees into Spain under cover of darkness because of the non-intervention policies of the British and French governments, volunteers in the thick of battles on various fronts, trains as hospitals, blood transfusion units and ambulances, and activities, after the International Brigades were withdrawn, to aid Spain, Basque children, reunions of the IBA and of memorials.

In the final days in Spain the International Brigaders pledged:

We are returning to our respective countries not for celebrations in our honour, not to rest, but to continue the fight we helped to wage in Spain. We are merely changing the fronts and the weapons.

The International Brigade Memorial Archive testifies to the fact that that pledge has been fulfilled to the hilt.

Transport House International Room, London

London

We who are left, how shall we look again
Happily on the sun or feel the rain
Without remembering how they who went
Ungrudgingly and spent
Their lives for us loved, too, the sun and rain?

Lines from a poem by the Northumbrian Wilfred Wilson Gibson (1878–1962), quoted by International Brigader Jack Jones in his autobiography *Union Man*, speak eloquently of the debt that is owed to those who sacrificed their lives in the anti-fascist cause in Spain so that democracy could breathe more freely for generations that followed.

The union that Jack Jones once led, Britain's largest, the Transport and General Workers' Union, acknowledged that debt to its numerous splendid members who fought so courageously in the International Brigade in Spain, some never to return.

At Transport House, new headquarters of the TGWU, 16 Palace Street, London SW1, there is a statuette with a plaque which has inscribed upon it: 'In tribute to the TGWU members who fought in defence of democracy in Spain 1936–1939. Voluntarios Internacionales de la Libertad.' It has an honoured place on a wall of what is known as the International Room with exhibits testifying to the union's long and great tradition of international solidarity.

The memorial, designed and made by the Liverpool sculptor Arthur Dooley, is based on his magnificent International Brigade memorial in Glasgow. Its smaller scale accentuates the vulnerability of the solitary figure. It was originally unveiled in June 1990 in the former TGWU headquarters in Smith Square, when the International Lounge was formally opened by Jack Jones at the invitation of the then general secretary, Ron Todd. The opening ceremony was attended by veteran International Brigaders Frank Deegan and Michael O'Riordan and TGWU executive officers, and the ceremenony was beamed by special video link to invited guests, including the executive in Transport Hall.

Jack Jones, born and raised in Garston, Liverpool, was secretary of his local Labour Party at fifteen, elected to the T&G branch committee at twenty-one, a year later was on the union's national dock committee and at twenty-four was elected a Liverpool city councillor. He describes in his autobiography the sympathetic response from working people and large sections of liberal-minded opinion in the city to Spain. He spent a lot of his time organizing collections and meetings for Spain. After repeated attempts to be allowed to go out to Spain – he was told he was needed to organize union support for Spain in Liverpool – he eventually went and had a distinguished record of service.

He served as political commissar with the Major Attlee Company which was commanded by Paddy O'Daire, for whom Jack Jones had warm words of praise. He describes the crucial battle on the Ebro front for Hill 481,

Jack Jones with the Transport and General Workers' Union memorial at Transport House before it was installed in the International Room. The inscription on the plaque reads: 'In tribute to the TGWU members who fought in defence of democracy in Spain 1936–1939. Voluntarios Internacionales de la Libertad.'

known as the Pimple, which was critical for the prevention of the capture of Gandesa:

> German and Italian planes were bombing and strafing, while anti-aircraft opposition from our side hardly existed . . . Day after day we made attacks on Hill 481 to try to gain the summit, an almost impossible task without artillery and air support. The fascists had placed concrete pill-boxes and machine guns in key positions commanding every approach to the summit. Mines had been tied to bushes; if you touched one you were blown to pieces . . . the number of dead and wounded mounted rapidly.

Paddy O'Daire instructing a Spanish lieutenant with the British Battalion in grenade throwing.

He himself became a casualty, wounded in the shoulder and right arm. 'Blood gushed from my shoulder and I couldn't lift my rifle. I could do nothing but lie where I was. Near me a comrade had been killed and I could hear the cries of others, complaining of their wounds.' His right arm was hit again, by a spray of shrapnel. He had to be taken to hospital and was then repatriated.

After years as his union's leader in Coventry and the West Midlands he was elected general secretary in 1968 and led the union for nine years, holding many prominent positions in the TUC and was a principal spokesman on international and economic matters. On retirement he became as well known as a tireless fighter for pensioners.

The esteem in which Jack Jones was held by the labour and trade union movement was illustrated by the great eightieth birthday salute to him held in Congress House in March 1993 when the Dowlais Male Voice Choir performed. Speeches were made by the then Labour leader John Smith, TUC president Dan Duffy, TGWU general secretary Bill Morris and Bill Alexander on behalf of the International Brigade Association.

It is one of the tragedies of war that it is not always possible to keep accurate records of those who fought and those who perished, but among TGWU volunteers killed in Spain were: London bus driver Bill Briskey in February 1937 at Jarama, building worker George Brown of Manchester at Brunete in July 1937, and Ken Bond of London at Ebro in July 1938.

André Malraux (1901–76), French Resistance leader, in his *Days of Hope* spoke of such heroes:

> So they came in long columns from all countries, all who knew poverty well enough to die fighting it, and some had guns and those who had no guns used their hands, and one after another they came to lie down on the earth of Spain.

Unity Theatre, St Pancras, London

London

People of England, while you ponder,
The ring is closing, the iron ring that strangles us . . .
Hear it . . . The voice of the people crying to the people:
Today it is us: Tomorrow it will be you.
People of England, what are you going to do?

These lines are from the poem *Spain* by communist writer Randall Swingler, which was performed as a mass declamation by London's Unity Theatre in 1936. As Colin Chambers relates in his *Story of Unity Theatre*, solidarity with the young Spanish Republic fighting for its life became the driving force of much that the theatre did at that time, so forging strong ties with the International Brigade.

Unity was founded in 1936 as an unashamedly partisan and propagandist theatre of working people. It produced plays about the struggles of the working class in language accessible to it, often spontaneous and performed mainly by untrained people. However, it proved an excellent training ground for some highly successful professionals.

Unity revived Ramon Sender's Spanish play, *The Secret*, to raise funds for Spain. John Allen and Margaret Leona turned Jack Lindsay's *On Guard for Spain* into a powerful mass declamation for Unity. The theatre staged the first performance in Britain of Brecht's *Mrs Carrar's Rifles*, with its Spanish theme, in a new translation by the director, Herbert Marshall, and Freda Brilliant. *Mrs Carrar's Rifles* and *On Guard for Spain* were performed at numerous meetings and rallies all over Britain.

Unity played at an International Brigade reunion at St Pancras Town Hall in October 1938 and helped stage a Welcome Home Pageant in January 1939 at the Empress Hall in honour of volunteers returning from Spain. In 1943 Unity's mobile group commemorated the Battle of Jarama with a play, *We Fight On*, at the Scala Theatre in the West End under the auspices of the International Brigade Association. Written by J.S. Frieze it recounts in thirteen scenes the story of the volunteers from 1936 to 1943. This required a cast and choir of 150, drawn from exiled Free Austrian, Free German, Czechoslovak and Spanish Republican cultural groups. Unity Theatre president Ted Willis's *All One Battle* was performed in 1945 at the Coliseum for the International Brigade, showing that those who had fought in Spain continued the same struggle in Italy, Yugoslavia, the Soviet Union and Japan, and later in Spain itself. The following year saw Unity stage International Brigader George Leeson's play, *The Trampled Earth*, about the plight of Republicans in Franco's gaols.

A founder member of Unity Theatre, Edward Burke (whose real name was Cooper, but known at Unity as Henry), was a professional actor and producer associated with the Royal Shakespeare Company and Left Theatre. He became Unity's first producer, bringing to bear his extensive experience in the theatre's early shows. A stalwart anti-fascist in his student days, he spoke at a Trafalgar Square rally for Spain and was one of the first to volunteer, leaving for Spain the day after the historic Cable Street battle against Mosley's Blackshirts. In September 1936 he joined the Tom Mann Centuria in Spain. He was one of the volunteers who fought in the early battles to save Madrid. He died at the Córdoba front in February 1937 at the age of twenty-six from wounds he received. A memorial evening was staged for him by the Unity Theatre Club in February 1938. His colleagues eventually erected a memorial plaque to him at Unity Theatre in Goldington Street, St Pancras – which must have been destroyed when Unity Theatre was burnt down in 1975.

George Leeson, who became Unity's general manager in the 1950s, was taken prisoner fighting with the machine-gun company at Jarama in February 1937. With a number of other volunteers he was tried at Salamanca and sentenced to death by a military court. When a group of British volunteers was exchanged for fascist officers, George Leeson and Morry Goldberg, a clothing worker from Stepney, were kept back, probably for no other reason than the regime's anti-semitism. George Leeson was eventually released after a campaign and questions being raised in Parliament, but Morry Goldberg was detained for another two months.

Unity actors Ben Glaser, a tailor from Stepney and former member of Rebel Players, and Bruce Boswell, from Coventry, who also volunteered to join the International Brigade, both wrote letters to Unity from Spain. In one Bruce Boswell said he and Ben Glaser formed a Unity group called the

The cover of the original 1938 Memorial Meeting programme to honour Henry Burke.

The official confirmation of Edward Burke's death from the International Brigade Base, Albacete, dated 10 September 1937, which reads:

*To Comrade Adam
Mrs Cooper, mother of our late comrade Cooper Edward Henry Burke, has asked us for details about the death of her son, we ask you to communicate to her the following: Comrade Burke died on 12/2/37 at the Federal Hospital following a wound to his stomach.
He is interred at the Cemetery of the East in Madrid. The address to write to is:
Mrs Cooper, The Grange, Dunstow, Oxon, England.
Anti-fascist greetings
The Chief of the Service Research Office.*

People's Theatre and put on a concert a few miles from where guns were blazing in Chabolla Valley – a chabolla was a bush shelter constructed from the branches of hazelnut bushes that covered the valley. The British Battalion was resting and training there for the final assault across the Ebro, where Bruce Boswell was killed in July and Ben Glaser in September 1938.

The entrance and the Unity Theatre building in the background in Goldington Street, St Pancras, London, before it was burnt down.

Camden Town Hall, London

Do not go gentle into that good night,
Old age should burn and rave at close of day;
Rage, rage against the dying of the light.

Dylan Thomas

London

These lines applied in all their fullness to the veterans of the British Battalion who fought in Spain, all in their eighties, in whom the flame of liberty and anti-fascism still burned so fiercely in 1995. They came together on 29 April in Camden, north London to honour their comrades who fought in Spain, especially those who never returned.

The occasion was the unveiling of a plaque which

commemorates the volunteers who set off from this borough
to fight in the International Brigades: Spain 1936–1939
and also those citizens of this borough who supported
the Spanish Republic in its fight against fascism
No Pasaran!

It was a solemn and emotional moment when veteran Wally Togwell, erect, carried the battered British Battalion banner into the Town Hall, followed by the Camden Mayor, Billy Budd, several other veterans, their supporters who had collected money, food and medical supplies for the

Patience Edney and Wally Togwell stand with their memories and the British Battalion banner before the memorial plaque to their comrades and supporters.

THIS PLAQUE COMMEMORATES
THE VOLUNTEERS WHO SET OFF
FROM THIS BOROUGH TO FIGHT IN
THE INTERNATIONAL BRIGADES
SPAIN, 1936~1939
AND ALSO THOSE CITIZENS
OF THIS BOROUGH WHO SUPPORTED
THE SPANISH REPUBLIC
IN ITS FIGHT AGAINST FASCISM

¡NO PASARAN!

Donated by the People of Camden
Unveiled by the Mayor, Councillor Bill Budd
29 April 1995

The memorial plaque designed by Mike Jones.

Spanish people nearly sixty years earlier, and their friends. They had come from all parts of London.

Unveiling the plaque, the mayor recalled how he had tried to volunteer for the International Brigade, but was told that at sixteen he was too young. The beautifully designed and highly polished stainless steel plaque was the work of artist Mike Jones.

Wally Togwell first raised the need for a memorial in a letter to the *Camden New Journal*, and it became a reality through the efforts of a number of people like veteran International Brigade nurse Patience Edney, Avis Hutt who campaigned for the cause of Spain in the thirties, and Camden councillors Anne Swain and Gerry Harrison. Over £1,000 was collected towards the cost of the plaque.

There was widespread support in the Camden area in the thirties for the Spanish Republican cause. Local anti-fascists like Wally Togwell helped to break up Oswald Mosley's Blackshirt meetings. He remembered William Joyce (Lord Haw Haw) speaking from an armoured van and fighting in the streets. Shoppers at the large local Co-operative store opposite Camden Town tube station used to fill a large dustbin every week with tins of milk and other foodstuffs for shipment to Spain.

Twenty-three volunteers from Camden went to fight alongside the Spanish people, ten of whom died on the battlefields of Spain.

A large number of Cypriots had settled in London to escape from the poverty of the British colony. In the thirties they worked in the hotels and restaurants of the West End and many lived in the area between Euston Road and Camden Town. True to the best traditions of their Greek forefathers, the heroes of the Greek War of Independence, the Cypriots, who were also convinced anti-fascists, rallied to support the young Spanish republic. Many from the Camden Town area went to fight in Spain in the International Brigade, some never to return. Altogether fourteen Cypriots were killed in Spain. Many held very senior positions – people like Hercules Avgherinos, Evanthis Nicolaides (who came to Spain from the Soviet Union) and Michael Economides, who was one of those who returned. He was present at the unveiling ceremony at Camden Town Hall. A company political commissar with the British Battalion, he fought in Spain for two and a half years and was wounded in the Gandesa battle.

The first English person to fire a rifle at Franco's rebelling troops and to be killed in Spain was sculptor Felicia Browne, a 32-year-old graduate of the Slade and other art schools. She was a truly gifted young woman who was remarkably clear intellectually about why she was fighting in Spain. She wrote to a friend before she went to Spain: 'You say I am escaping and evading things by not painting or making sculpture. If there is no painting or sculpture to be made, I cannot make it. . . . If painting and sculpture were more valid or urgent to me than the earthquake which is happening in the revolution. . . . I should paint or make sculpture.' She joined the militia in Barcelona on 2 August 1936, went with a group to Aragon, and was killed twenty-three days later when rescuing a fellow fighter who had been wounded on patrol.

Patience Edney (née Darton) came from a staunchly Tory family but began to think critically about politics through church discussion groups. She was affected by the awful poverty she saw in south London homes. Directed to Medical Aid, she was asked to fly out to Spain to nurse the seriously wounded British Battalion commander Tom Wintringham. She quickly healed him by completely changing his treatment and after a period at the Valencia fever hospital was sent to Polenino. Later she joined Dr Crome's unit on the other side of the Ebro and saw service in other areas in Spain, having to work under deplorable conditions and with poor equipment.

At the unveiling ceremony Patience Edney remarked that those who took part in the struggle against fascism alongside the Spanish people were 'a part of history, and that should never be forgotten'.

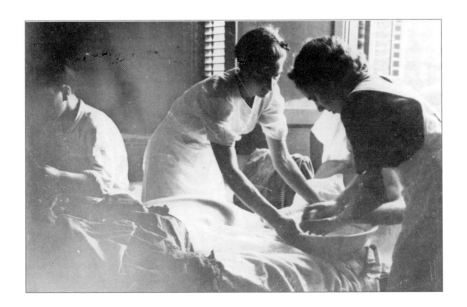

Patience Edney (facing camera) training a Spanish nurse in a hospital in Spain.

Southwark Town Hall, London

For the war in Spain is war for the human future
All that crawls evil of the holes of the past
and all that rises with love for the lucid warmth of the day
meet in this grapple. In it meet
the evil and the good that swarm
in your inherited blood
Yes, yours and yours, and yours.

The extract above comes from *On Guard for Spain* written by Jack Lindsay in 1937, performed as a mass recitation by London's Unity Theatre and chosen by the London Borough of Southwark in November 1986 for its folder announcing the unveiling of a plaque in Southwark Town Hall in the presence of the Mayor of Southwark, Jessie Cannon, to commemorate those from the borough who volunteered for the International Brigade.

The lines eloquently express both how Spain caught the imagination of progressives and how well its significance was understood by them. The reactionary Catholic Action which supported Franco was very influential in Bermondsey and North Peckham, but there was also a strong democratic and anti-fascist current which inspired collections of food and funds for medicines for Spain. The Camberwell Young Communist League had a trumpet band with which they toured the streets around Heaton Arms with coster barrows borrowed from the Choumart Road market. People brought to their doors by the drum beats would hasten back with tins of milk, beans, peas and packets of tea and sugar.

London Borough of Southwark Mayor Rita Sergeant shaking hands with Lt.-Gen. Alexander Osipenko in July 1988 in the Town Hall in front of the Borough's memorial to the International Brigaders.

Thirteen people from Southwark fought in the International Brigade; four of them were killed in the fighting.

One of the thirty-three British veterans of the International Brigade from Greater London invited to the unveiling ceremony was Margaret Russell, née Powell. She was one of the outstanding nurses who went to Spain. Daughter of Welsh hill-farmers in the Black Mountains, she and her three sisters all trained as nurses. Margaret Powell was one of the first to join a trade union. She volunteered for Spain as soon as the conflict started there. Advised to first finish her midwifery course, she travelled out to Spain in early 1937. She was created a Dame of the Order of Loyalty to the Spanish Republic for her 'valiant action as a nurse . . . her faith, self-sacrifice and devotion to our wounded and to our war victims'. She was one of the last nurses to leave Spain. Having lost her passport she was arrested by the French police and was eventually rescued by a Quaker relief team.

British nurses Margaret Powell (second left), Mary Slater (third left) and Annie Murray (centre) in Spain with medical staff.

Sam Lesser (he wrote under the name Sam Russell), who married Margaret Powell in later years, another of those invited to the ceremony, was one of the first small group of British volunteers to fight in Spain, in particular in the successful defence of Madrid. He and his comrades helped to boost the morale of the citizens of Madrid, showing them they were not alone, when they rallied to defend their city against the superior

THIS PLAQUE WAS ERECTED BY THE COUNCIL OF THE LONDON BOROUGH OF SOUTHWARK, TO COMMEMORATE THOSE RESIDENTS OF SOUTHWARK, BERMONDSEY AND CAMBERWELL WHO FOUGHT WITH THE INTERNATIONAL BRIGADE IN THE SPANISH CIVIL WAR.

BILL ALEXANDER	PAUL DEWHURST	JIM HOY
CONSTANTINE AUGHERINOS	DOUGAL EGGAR	JACK L. JONES
HARRY BOURNE	HARRY EVANS	LOU KENTON
JOCK CUNNINGHAM	JOE FUHR	JOHN RIORDAN
LEN CROME	DAVE GIBBONS	TED SMITH
MARGARET POWELL (NURSE)	GEORGE HARDY	
HERACLES AUGHERINOS		

UNVEILED BY THE MAYOR OF SOUTHWARK, COUNCILLOR JESSIE CANNON ON 6 NOVEMBER 1986.

The memorial plaque in the Mayor's Parlour, Southwark Town Hall.

fascist forces of Franco. Lesser was wounded at Lopera. As a London student he had been very active in the battles against Mosley's Blackshirts. He worked with a Spanish news agency, helping to send regular reports to the *Daily Worker* and other English-language journals and became the paper's correspondent in Spain after Peter Kerrigan. In the 1950s he was the paper's Moscow correspondent, returning to London to serve as the Foreign Editor of the paper and its successor, the *Morning Star*.

Len Crome (right) supervising the arrival of bedding for the wounded.

Dr Len Crome, also a veteran living in the area, served in the medical services of the International Brigade, reaching the highest rank, Officer-in-Command of Medical Services of the 35th International Division and later Officer-in-Command of Medical Services of the 5th Army Corps. His family had emigrated from Latvia in 1926 when he was seventeen. He did his medical training in Edinburgh. He had been a young doctor working in a hospital in Blackburn, Lancashire, when he heard volunteers were needed in Spain. Though a member of the Left Book Club, he was not active politically but he wrote to Harry Pollitt about going out to Spain. He was advised that he should apply to the Scottish Ambulance unit. He developed exceptional organizational abilities in Spain, playing an important role not only in developing the medical services, but also in reassuring the wounded. His experience in organizing medical services in the anti-fascist war was studied and followed by many armies in the Second World War. After the war he worked as a GP in Southwark and later became a consultant. For many years he has served as the chairman of the International Brigade Association.

In July 1988 Lt.-Gen. Osipenko, a Hero of the Soviet Union, chairman of the Soviet War Veterans (Spanish section) and Soviet International Brigade veteran met some of Southwark's surviving Brigade veterans when he was received by the Mayor, Rita Sergeant, and inspected the commemorative plaque in the Town Hall. As a young fighter pilot he volunteered and served in the Spanish Republican Air Force while young Spanish pilots were being trained in the USSR. During the Second World War he commanded the 5th Air Army of the Soviet Airforce based in the far north. His fighter planes patrolled out at sea to give cover to British and US convoys taking supplies to Murmansk. During his visit to Britain he spoke at the Jubilee Gardens International Brigade memorial and gave a lecture in Manchester where he was received by the lord mayor and took part in a ceremony at the memorial plaque in the Town Hall.

St Luke's Church, Peckham, London

London

San Pedro was a two-hundred-year-old convent crammed to the very last inch with six hundred or so International Brigaders of every nationality, who were kept apart from the several thousand Spanish prisoners. Here the efforts to break and intimidate the men sank to new depths of sadism. They slept on the floor in long rooms, literally shoulder to shoulder, with very little light or ventilation. It was stifling in summer but freezing cold in the depth of winter. There were three taps to provide water for drinking and washing for all the prisoners. . . . The lavatories were open, of the crudest style, and were often blocked. Lice, dysentery, rheumatism and skin diseases affected everyone. The food, mainly beans and a little bread, was barely sufficient to keep men alive, and was often bad, and not properly cooked. Many of the wounded had been shot on the spot when captured, but those with minor wounds received no special treatment.

This extract from Bill Alexander's book British Volunteers for Liberty describes the conditions endured by Douglas Copplestone Eggar, the oldest British prisoner in San Pedro and in Palencia concentration camps.

He arrived in Spain in 1937, attached to the 35th division of the 15th Brigade. While Hitler and Mussolini were supplying Franco's fascist forces with modern weapons, tanks and aircraft, the Republican forces and the International Brigades were denied any such help because of the calculated one-sided policy of Non-Intervention adopted by Britain and France. Douglas Eggar described how they 'were dreadfully short of armaments. The situation was so bad that on one occasion we were issued with rifles one day and ordered to give them up the next because they had to be passed on to a Czechoslovak brigade which was going into action that day and had no weapons whatsoever.'

He was taken prisoner along with many other British volunteers when they were ambushed by an armoured column of Mussolini's regular armed forces. On capture, like many of his comrades, he was threatened with death – some were shot in cold blood. But the fascists were unable to break his spirit. He was able to withstand everything and help others because of his convictions – political and religious – and because of the mutual solidarity of the prisoners. He and other British prisoners were eventually exchanged for Italian soldiers captured by the Republican forces.

Douglas Eggar died in April 1992, after moving into sheltered accommodation where he won great respect and admiration, testified to by the celebration party for his ninetieth birthday. The Battalion banner covered his coffin at his funeral service in his church, St Luke's in Peckham, which was attended by many of his neighbours, fellow churchgoers and eight International Brigaders. 'The Valley of Jarama' was sung.

The Red Stole with the IBA symbol in memory of
Douglas Eggar, being worn by Revd Andrew Davey
of St Luke's Church.

Douglas Eggar was a unique man with many and varied talents – he was a painter, boxer, a Bevin Boy and writer. Above all he was a committed anti-fascist, a communist and sincere Christian.

St Luke's Church commissioned the Red Stole (clergy scarf) in memory of Douglas Eggar to be worn on St Luke's Day – 18 October – and on other martyrs' days, Palm Sunday and Pentecost. It was designed and made by Juliet Hemingray of Derby. It is a glorious red stole with the IBA symbol in prominence opposite the Holy Trinity. The symbols of suffering – chains and barbed wire – are fragmented and broken, there are also thorns – symbols of martyrdom – surrounded by the pentecostal flames of the Holy Spirit.

Douglas Eggar with his beloved dog Casper, surrounded by friends at his ninetieth birthday celebration.

Aberdeen

There was a tremendous anti-fascist feeling in Aberdeen, as there was throughout the whole country . . . when the Spanish Civil War broke out in July 1936, we thought it was going to be precisely that – a Spanish Civil War. But later on, round about December when tales were coming back about the intervention by Hitler and Mussolini in Spain, it ceased to be a Spanish Civil War. . . . It was now a war of intervention . . . we thought that if we were going to be anti-fascist in the real sense of the word it was our job to try and help as far as we possibly could . . . the fight, whether it be here in Aberdeen against the British Union of Fascists or against Hitler and Mussolini in Spain, was exactly the same fight to me.

This is John Londragan explaining why he and seventeen other Aberdonians decided they had to volunteer to go to Spain in 1937. The extract comes from *Voices from the Spanish Civil War*, a collection of personal recollections of Scottish volunteers.

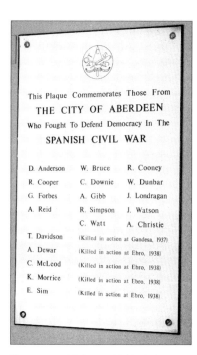

The two memorial plaques with identical inscriptions – one in the foyer of the Aberdeen Concert Hall, the other at the Aberdeen Trades Council Club.

There are two identical bronze plaques in Aberdeen, one in the foyer of the Concert Hall and another at the Aberdeen Trades Council Club, which commemorate 'Those from the City of Aberdeen who fought to defend Democracy in the Spanish Civil War.' They bear the names of the thirteen volunteers who returned and the five who were killed on the battlefields of Spain.

Aberdeen Unemployment Centre, at 54 Frederick Street, was set up in 1989 to provide business and trade training. There is a very real connection between the Unemployment Centre and the war in Spain. In the depression of the thirties the British Union of Fascists tried hard to recruit the unemployed, but out-of-work Aberdonians wanted no part of them. The attempts to build Mosley's party in Aberdeen were vigorously opposed and defeated. In October 1934 Aberdeen communists staged a demonstration against fascists who were attempting to hold a meeting in Castle Street – a number of arrests followed with the press describing the confrontation as a 'riot'. These attempts to build Mosley's party failed as the anti-fascists were well organized – drivers and conductors informed them where the fascists were likely to assemble so that they could be harried. Often demonstrators were baton-charged by police, arrests were made and people imprisoned.

The 15th International Brigade Aberdeen Memorial Library plaque with the IBA symbol.

So it was very appropriate that a few months after its establishment the Unemployment Centre held a ceremony for an official opening and dedication of the Aberdeen Memorial Library to the 15th International Brigade. An

Bill Alexander with a group of veterans examining some of the books collected for the Aberdeen Memorial Library, then housed in the Aberdeen Unemployment Centre in Frederick Street. John Londragan is standing on the right with an open book.

impressive exhibition of photographs and newspaper cuttings was mounted along one wall with the slogan 'No Pasaran!' above in red letters. Draped on one side was the Spanish Republican flag with the words: 'From the Aberdeen Boys Fighting in Spain.' Present at the ceremony were a number of veterans of the International Brigade who were greeted by Lord Provost of Aberdeen Robert Robertson. John Londragan, the sole survivor of the Aberdeen volunteers, opened the library, saying it was a 'magnificent memorial'.

The library contains books donated by anti-fascists and Brigade members and includes poetry composed by men who fought in Spain. It was established with help from the Aberdeen City District Council, local trade unions and businesses.

There is in existence a copy of a very moving letter from an Aberdonian volunteer, Bob Cooney, from the front in Spain to the daughter of Aberdonian Tom Davidson. He wrote:

We went into action again on Thursday, March 31st near the small village of Calaceite where we were ambushed by Italian tanks and infantry. We suffered terrific losses and by the end of the day we were reduced to a handful. . . . Your father was one of the first to volunteer for the job of holding a hill near the Calaceite–Caspe–Gandesa cross-roads. The defence of that hill held the fascists for 24 hours but on the following night we had

A break during the Ebro offensive. Bob Cooney sitting next to George Fletcher, an expert machine gunner and one of the British Battalion commanders, and behind them, Peter Kerrigan, Daily Worker correspondent in Spain.

to withdraw as we were outflanked. We withdrew as far as the cross-roads where we formed patrols to prevent the fascists from using the roads and bringing up their armour. Your father had so impressed everyone by his coolness and courage under fire that he was placed in charge of one of the patrols. . . . When we reached Gandesa we found the fascists in occupation and we had to fight our way through the town. It was here that your father was killed . . . That rearguard action by halting the fascists at the Ebro enabled the Republic to resist for another year. Your father was modest as he was brave and you may well be proud of him.

It was typical of the thoughtfulness and compassion displayed by Bob Cooney, who helped to keep a daily diary of the British Battalion in Spain. Because of his responsibilities as a communist leader in Aberdeen, he was first refused clearance to go to Spain and had to make special representation to be allowed to go. In Spain he became a company commissar. As a consequence of the political leadership he displayed in battles such as at Calaceite, he was one of those appointed as battalion political commissar, a responsibility he carried out in an exemplary manner, complementing the leadership of his battalion commander.

Following his death a memorial concert evening to Bob Cooney was held in November 1989 at the Aberdeen TUC Club. Such was the esteem in which he was held that poets and folk-singers from all over the Highlands came to celebrate and honour his life and contribution to the fight for liberty and democracy.

John Londragan also displayed sterling qualities in Spain. After training at Madrigueras he became No. 1 in an anti-tank unit and was wounded on the Brunete front when the British Battalion was trying to take the crucial Mosquito Ridge where the fascist forces were holed up. As John Londragan explained: 'This finished my career as regards the anti-tank.' He left Spain minus a finger and with head and leg injuries. That did not deter him from serving with the British Army in the Second World War. 'I went through the Second World War doing exactly the same job I went to Spain to do. . . .Both were anti-fascist wars,' he said.

The plaque naming Aberdeen Trades Council headquarters John Londragan House.

When he died in 1993, Aberdeen Trades Council named its refurbished headquarters John Londragan House in recognition of his life-long commitment to trade unionism and in remembrance of his bravery during the anti-fascist war in Spain.

Trades Council president Jurgen Thomaneck declared: 'If ever there was a working-class hero in Aberdeen . . . it was Johnny Londragan.'

Customs House Quay, Glasgow

Glasgow

But if things wur bad in the Calton they wur worse elsewhere. Franco in the middle. Mussolini oan the right-wing. Hitler waitin tae come oan. When they three goat thegithir an came up against the Spanish workers, they didnae expect the Calton tae offer handers . . . The Blackshirts, the Brownshirts, the Blueshirts, fascists of every colour and country came up against the men and women ae no mean city, against grey simmets an bunnets an headscarfs, against troosers tied wae string and shoes that let the rain in, against guns that were auld enough tae remember Waterloo. Fae nae hair tae grey hair they answered the call. Many never came back. They wur internationalists. They wur Europeans. They wur Scots. Glasgow should be proud ae them!

This is the 'Chorus' which opens *Calton to Catalonia*, a prison drama set during the war in Spain and based partly on the experiences of volunteers from Glasgow, including Calton-born James Maley, the father of the authors, John and Willy.

James Maley was taken prisoner at Jarama in February 1937 and had to endure terrible conditions for five months in captivity. His mother picked him out when she watched a Movietone newsreel and was able to persuade the projectionist at the cinema to cut a couple of frames from the newsreel. This inspired the idea for the play, which was first performed during Glasgow's year as the European City of Culture in December 1990 in the Lithgow Theatre, Govan, to enthusiastic notices in *The Scotsman*, the *Glasgow Herald* and the *Evening Times*.

Solidarity was born of the poverty, hardship and unemployment that characterized life in the thirties in Glasgow and elsewhere in the British Isles and out of solidarity grew resistance, Hunger Marches from one end of the country to the other and resistance to home-grown fascists trying exploit the situation. That solidarity reached physically out to Spain when democratic republican forces came under attack from Franco and his allies, Hitler and Mussolini.

Garry McCartney who had his baptism of fire on the Aragon front, went through the battle at Teruel and was captured at Calaceite. Interviewed in *Voices*, he said: 'The working class movement in Glasgow was very much informed and very involved in the anti-fascist struggle. Glasgow at the weekend was a forum of meetings, all over the city, at street corners and in the centre of the city.'

One of the first to go to Spain from Scotland was Young Communist League member Phil Gillan, born in 1912 in the Gorbals. Like others of his generation he was unemployed in the 1920s and '30s, became a member of the National Unemployed Workers' Movement and played a side-drum in the Gorbals Unemployed Flute Band. Phil Gillan was one of the small band of British volunteers who went into battle with the Spanish people to prevent Madrid falling to Franco's forces in 1937.

Some of the supporters at the Glasgow memorial after its unveiling on 23 February 1980 at the Clyde Walkway, Customs House Quay. Below the figure of La Pasionaria are inscribed her words: 'Better to die on your feet than to live forever on your knees.' The inscription on the plaque below reads: 'The City of Glasgow and the British Labour Movement pay tribute to the courage of those men and women who went to Spain to fight Fascism 1936–1939. 2,100 Volunteers went from Britain 534 were killed 53 of whom were from Glasgow.'

A group of confident volunteers from Scotland.

On 23 February 1980 the City of Glasgow honoured the volunteers from Glasgow and district who went out to fight alongside the Spanish people in the International Brigade, sixty-five of whom died in Spain.

Glasgow Lord Provost David Hodge, watched by some 400 people, including some forty members of the British Battalion and representatives of the Scottish labour, trade union and progressive movements, unveiled a permanent memorial to the volunteers on the city centre's riverside, the Clyde Walkway, Customs House Quay.

The powerful bronze memorial made by sculptor Arthur Dooley represents the defiant figure with head held back and arms stretching up of Spain's anti-fascist leader Dolores Ibarruri – La Pasionaria. The sculpture carries the inspiring advice she gave to the Spanish people when Franco generals rebelled against the newly elected popular government in 1936: 'Better to die on your feet than to live forever on your knees.'

Arthur Dooley, who hailed from Liverpool, studied art by first taking a job sweeping up in London's St Martin's School of Art. His first one-man show was at the St Martin's Gallery. A colourful character, who preferred working with scrap metal or bronze, he had little sympathy with the London art scene and its art schools. The BBC made a film, *The Modern Passion*, about Arthur Dooley and his outstanding work *Stations of the Cross* at St Mary's in Leyland, Lancashire, which won international prizes. When he made the Glasgow memorial sculpture, it was so big that he could not get it through the doors and there was nothing for it but to remove a section of the wall. Arthur Dooley died in January 1994, aged sixty-four.

Baillieston Public Library, Glasgow

A t Baillieston, Glasgow, two school students, Lorraine Devine and David Hill, studied the anti-fascist war in Spain as part of their school project. In December 1989 they read short extracts from their studies at a ceremony to honour a son of their former mining village – William Keegan, who was killed at Brunete in 1937 at the age of twenty-eight while fighting with the International Brigade.

The two teenagers proudly stood on one side as Glasgow Lord Provost Susan Baird unveiled the memorial plaque in the Baillieston Public Library to William Keegan – the torch of democracy and liberty that he and his fellow volunteers had carried fifty years earlier had passed into their young hands to keep alight.

William Keegan was a jobless miner, a communist active in the unemployed workers' movement. Before he volunteered and set off with three bus-loads of fellow volunteers to Spain he had been active in raising funds for Spain, persuading hundreds of working people like himself to part with their Co-op dividends to help the Spanish people.

Glasgow

School students Lorraine Devine and David Hill by the memorial plaque to William Keegan after it was unveiled in the Baillieston Public Library by Glasgow Lord Provost Susan Baird in December 1989.

Fifty years later a National Union of Public Employees shop steward and miner's widow Lizzie Martin remembered seeing William Keegan setting off and told her son-in-law, Strathclyde regional Labour councillor Douglas Hay (a joiner), about it and he put the wheels in motion to have a memorial erected to William Keegan. He and sheetmetal worker Willie Gibson, a full-time union official, returned to their respective trades to make the plaque. They raised the funds by public subscription for the memorial, involving Strathclyde and Glasgow council leaders, and the local labour and trade union movement.

Present at the ceremony were the brother and sister of William Keegan and International Brigade veterans Phil Gillan and James Maley, along with representatives of the Scottish Trade Union Congress, National Union of Mineworkers and community groups.

Baillieston district was once a North Lanarkshire mining village and many young miners from the area went to fight in Spain with the International Brigade and all together eleven of them gave their lives in Spain.

Among them was Charles Goodfellow, a miner from Bellshill who, held in high regard for his coolness under fire at Jarama, was appointed second-in-command of the British Battalion during the Brunete offensive by the Republican forces. He wrote home: 'The years in the last war were nothing to this, but I know I am on the right side this time, and that we are making history that will inspire the workers of the whole world.'

Charles Goodfellow, 'a miner from Bellshill . . . held in high regard for his coolness under fire. . .'.

REPÚBLICA ESPAÑOLA
15.ª BRIGADA INTERNACIONAL
ESTADO MAYOR

O F F I C I A L   C E R T I F I C A T E   O F   D E A T H

We regret to announce that W.Keegan,

of 110, Bredicholme, Bailleston, Nr Glasgow.

was killed in action / died of wounds received on 18th day of

July 1937, while serving with the British Battalion

of the 15th. INTERNATIONAL BRIGADE at Brunete, Madrid. Spain.

His loss is mourned by all heroic anti-fascist fighters

serving with the INTERNATIONAL BRIGADES in Spain.

POLITICAL COMMISSAR

24th day, of July. 1937.

William Keegan's certificate of death.

Edinburgh

Edinburgh

For the first time in the history of the people's struggles, there has been the spectacle, breath taking in its grandeur, of the formation of International Brigades to help to save a threatened country's freedom and independence, the freedom and independence of our Spanish land. They gave us everything; their youth or their maturity; their science or their experience; their blood and their lives; their hopes and aspirations . . . and they asked us for nothing at all . . .

Dolores Ibarruri, La Pasionaria, in Barcelona in 1938 saluting the international volunteers who perished on Spanish soil and those about to return to their own countries. She eloquently summed up the magnificence of the sacrifice made by men and women to confront fascism.

Forty-two years on, her passionate words found an echo in Edinburgh at the unveiling of the Memorial Stone erected in the city's East Princes

Street Gardens to commemorate those who went from the city to serve in the International Brigade. A number of veteran volunteers, Scottish Labour MPs and representatives of the local labour and trade union movement were present at the unveiling ceremony.

A memorial fund of £1,500 from donations from all democratic organizations and individuals was established by the local International Brigade Association for the erection of the memorial in Edinburgh and also one in Fife. The appeal was sponsored by Lord Ritchie-Calder, nine MPs, eighteen local councillors and a number of other prominent Scottish people. The cooperation of the Edinburgh District Council was instrumental in having the Memorial Stone erected.

There is in addition a plaque in the Edinburgh Labour Party rooms with the simple inscription: 'In memory of those who left this city to serve with the International Brigade in the Spanish Civil War – Edinburgh City Labour Party.'

International Brigade veterans John Dunlop (with beret) and Steve Fullarton admire the memorial plaque in Edinburgh's East Princes Street Gardens, which carries the inscription:

To honour the memory of those who went
from the Lothians and Fife to serve in the
War in Spain 1936–1939

Not to a fanfare of trumpets,
Nor even the skirl of the pipes.
Not for the off'r of a shilling,
Nor to see their names up in lights.

Their call was a cry of anguish,
From the hearts of the people of Spain.
Some paid with their lives it is true;
Their sacrifice was not in vain.

Erected by
Friends of the International Brigade Association.

A fascist propaganda photograph showing British machine gunners captured at Jarama, 13 February 1937. Jim Rutherford (front row, first right) was shot in cold blood by his captors.

A number of Labour Party members from Edinburgh volunteered for the International Brigade. One of them was nineteen-year-old Jimmy Rutherford, member of the City's Labour League of Youth and Free Fishermen of Newhaven. With other members of the British Battalion, including Machine-Gun Company Commander Harold Fry, he was captured when they were surrounded on the second day of the Jarama Battle in February 1937. In the May they were released in exchange for fascist prisoners, but decided they must return to the British Battalion and within six weeks were back in Spain. Captured again, Jimmy Rutherford was recognized by a former fascist interrogator and executed in April 1938.

Jimmy Rutherford had met Harold Fry at an anti-fascist demonstration at Usher Hall, Edinburgh, where Mosley was trying to speak. He and Harold Fry were injured in the fray that followed – both needed stitches for split heads. He quotes Harold Fry as saying: 'Some day those bastards will provoke us into using rifles.' Harold Fry had served in the British Army in India and China, but after discharge became active in the working-class movement. Jimmy Rutherford, writing about his company commander, said: 'All through prison Fry gave us leadership and courage. Even when sentenced to death he maintained his calmness and cheeriness.' He became battalion commander, and was killed leading his men across no man's land in a barrage of artillery fire in October 1937 at Fuentes de Ebro.

Donald Renton, a well-known local Labour leader, was among those captured when their machine-gun company was surrounded and in Voices he recalled that the company 'at the beginning of that encirclement probably had around 120 men. When we finally were in fascist hands there were only some thirty of us left, the bulk of whom in one way or another had been knocked about rather badly. I'd been wounded in the legs, Harry Fry had a broken arm, shattered with machine gun bullets, Jimmy Rutherford was battered soft, George Watters had gone down.' Donald Renton was eventually repatriated and was put in charge of anti-fascist work in London's East End. He was a Labour councillor in Edinburgh from 1962 and died aged sixty-five in 1977.

Another Edinburgh Labour councillor Tom Murray was refused permission to go to Spain because of the importance of his political work as a councillor, but eventually went, taking part in the historic Ebro crossing. Two other members of his family also went, his brother George and sister Annie.

Donald Renton.

George (left) and Tom Murray in Spain.

Annie Murray gave distinguished service as a nurse in the medical unit at the front and became head nurse at the Huete base hospital. She described her feelings just after arrival in Spain:

> During the first attack I was on night duty and, because of this the war made a deep impression on my mind; for sick people are usually more ill at night, and our senses being more acute at night to the gruesomeness, the awful suffering of the men, especially those with abdominal wounds and haemorrhage for which one can do so little, became burnt on my mind. In those days many of the soldiers were under twenty years of age, and I shall never forget those young men with their bodies torn and their limbs smashed.

John Dunlop, born in Canada but brought up in Edinburgh, who joined the Communist Party just prior to the outbreak of the fascist Franco rebellion against the young Spanish Republic, also went to Spain and was wounded by a shell splinter in his back on the Brunete front.

Steve Fullarton and John Dunlop, two of the surviving Scottish veterans of the British Battalion gathered at the Memorial Stone in Princes Street Gardens in March 1993 to pay their respects to their former comrades in a simple ceremony with Edinburgh district councillors. John Dunlop declared: 'These men should not be forgotten. . . . They must not be forgotten for they gave their lives in defence of values which are under more bitter attack now all over the world than ever before.'

Annie Murray (left) with doctor and nurse at the Lerida front in 1938.

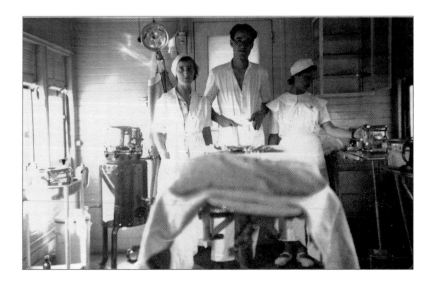

Forth Avenue North, Kirkcaldy, Fife

Kirkcaldy

Amid-thirties Aid to Spain meeting in the miners' institute in Valleyfield, Fife with just twelve people in the hall. Rab Smith says to Professor J.B.S. Haldane, treasurer of the Spanish Aid Fund and the main speaker: 'Look, there's hundreds through there in the games room. I'll go through and try to fetch them out.' Haldane replies: 'Twelve volunteers are better than a thousand conscripts.'

Rab Smith describes this episode in a booklet dedicated to the volunteers from Fife, published in 1986. He came from a small mining village, Lumphinnans, known as 'Little Moscow' in the 1930s, where poverty was rife but where concerts were held and collections made every week round the doors for Spain. He served in the International Brigade.

In the event thirty-seven Scots from the Fife area fought in Spain, where six of them were killed. Fife miner Hugh Sloan was one of the volunteers. An artist and working-class intellectual, he was said to have had the soul of a poet. On revisiting Spain in 1981 he was inspired to write a poem that explains why young people like him went to the aid of Spain:

> There was no other way we could go
> With idealism in our minds, we were no idealists
> With passion in our hearts, we were no romantics
> With fire in our bellies, we were no warriors
> We were doing the job that life had thrust upon us.

International Brigade veteran Tommy Bloomfield remembers his comrades whose names are inscribed on the plaque placed above the original memorial set in granite in the gardens at Forth Avenue North, Kirkcaldy, Scotland.

In May 1980 Friends of the International Brigade Association with the cooperation of Kirkcaldy District Council erected a stone memorial to commemorate those who went from the Lothians and Fife to Spain. It was erected in the gardens at Forth Avenue North, Kirkcaldy. The memorial carries an inscription, which in part reads:

> Their call was a cry of anguish
> From the hearts of the people of Spain.
> Some paid with their lives it is true;
> Their sacrifice was not in vain.

In September 1986 four men and one woman, the sole volunteer-survivors of the Spanish anti-fascist war walked erect through the crowd-filled Kirkcaldy streets when trade unionists, local councillors and the public saluted the International Brigaders.

A plaque was erected above the original memorial. It was sculpted by local artists Sandy Turner and Norman Higgins and bears the names of some of those who had volunteered and where they hailed from. It was unveiled by Councillor Robert Gough, convenor of Fife Regional Council.

Among the five survivors was Tommy Bloomfield who had been taken prisoner in Spain and kept in Franco's gaols for nearly four months. To him it seemed like years and he recalled that 'conditions were terrible. Some of us went back a second time because it made us more determined to fight the way we were treated.' He was overcome with emotion at the ceremony saying, 'People haven't forgotten us after all this time. They didn't die in vain.'

Present at the ceremony were representatives from the Fife branch of the Educational Institute of Scotland, the Transport and General Workers' Union, the Amalgamated Union of Engineering Workers, the Seafield branch of the National Union of Mineworkers, the Fire Brigades Union, the Kirkcaldy, Dundee and Clackmannan Trades Councils, the Levenmouth CND and Fife area of the Communist Party.

In March 1992 a moving ceremony sponsored by the Socialist Group of Euro MPs was held at the memorial to mark the 55th anniversary of the Battle of Jarama. Among those participating were Hugh Sloan, by then eighty, and Annie Knight, eighty-five, who had served with the International Brigade in Spain as a nurse.

She declared: 'We hope that the memory of our fight in Spain will inspire others to continue the fight against fascism, which is organising again throughout Europe.' They both laid wreaths at the memorial.

Dundee Peace Garden

Scotland made a significant contribution to the cause of Republican Spain, and Dundee was no exception. One hundred and twenty volunteers went from Dundee to fight in the International Brigade and seventeen of them were killed fighting on Spanish soil.

Dundee

There was poverty and no work in the late twenties and early thirties in Dundee as elsewhere. Many men joined the Territorial Army simply because it provided two weeks' paid holiday. But there was a fairly strong labour and trade union movement and an active Communist Party and Young Communist League. They helped to build a strong campaign for jobs under the umbrella of the National Unemployed Workers' Movement (NUWM).

Many men from Dundee took part in the historic 1934 Hunger March to London. It was this background together with the rise of Hitler in Germany, Mussolini in Italy and his invasion of Abyssinia that evoked such a powerful response when Franco led the rebellion against the young Spanish Republican Government.

In Dundee teachers and people in other professions played a leading part in organizing assistance to the hard-pressed Spanish people. The level of their activity can be judged from the fact that it resulted in two ambulances being sent to Spain from the town.

On 23 February 1975 the town honoured the volunteers who went to Spain by placing a metal plaque on a stone base in the Peace Garden, beside the Dundee Museum and Art Gallery in Albert Square.

It commemorates 'those who in the interests of democracy, served the cause of freedom in the International Brigade'. The ceremony was attended by Lord Provost Tom Moore and many veteran British Battalion volunteers, who proudly displayed the Scottish Committee British

The metal memorial plaque set on a granite stone base in the Peace Garden adjacent to the Dundee Museum and Art Gallery in Albert Square with the famous quotation from Nikolai Ostrovsky's book How the Steel was Tempered.

TO THE MEMORY OF THE DUNDEE MEMBERS
OF THE INTERNATIONAL BRIGADE
KILLED IN SPAIN FIGHTING FASCISM
1936 — 1938
— NO PASARAN —

JOHN TADDEN   KEN STALKER   WILLIAM McGUIRE   FRANK McCABE
JOHN McLANDERS   DAVE SAMSON   JAMES COCKBURN   JOHN ALEXANDER
MALCOLM SMITH   JOHN NESS   JOHN McEWEN   JOHN McHUGH
ANDREW FINNAN   JOHN MUDIE   JAMES MURRAY   MATT COX

MAN'S DEAREST POSSESSION IS LIFE AND SINCE
IT IS GRANTED TO LIVE BUT ONCE HE MUST SO
LIVE AS TO FEEL NO TORTURING REGRETS FOR
YEARS WITHOUT PURPOSE SO LIVE AS NOT TO
BE SEARED BY THE SHAME OF A COWARDLY AND
TRIVIAL PAST SO LIVE THAT DYING HE CAN
SAY ALL MY LIFE AND ALL MY STRENGTH WERE
GIVEN TO THE FINEST CAUSE IN THE WORLD —
THE FIGHT FOR THE LIBERATION OF MANKIND

Battalion Banner. They were entertained to a lunch at the Dundee Swimming and Leisure Centre following the ceremony.

Among the veterans was Frank McCusker who had worked in the local jute mill from the age of twelve to eighteen, when he was paid off soon after the General Strike of 1926. Apart from casual work he remained unemployed for many years and joined the Territorials. 'You got a fortnight's holiday and you got paid, and that's what I joined it for,' he explained. He was a member of the NUWM and one of the Hunger Marchers.

He took part in the Battle of Jarama. 'Well,' he said, 'it wasn't a battle at all, it was a bloody slaughter as far as we were concerned. They had everything and we had nothing. And that's where we lost the majority of our men . . . we lost about ten men from Dundee alone . . . the International Brigade got a real beating up there.' He was at Jarama for eight weeks and later took part in the fighting on the Brunete front and was wounded in the arm by an explosive bullet at Villanueva de la Canada. 'And I never saw any more fighting after that.' Gangrene set in and he was taken to a hospital in Madrid where he was operated on. He was transferred to one hospital after another during a period of a year and eventually when he arrived back in England he was operated on at the Middlesex Hospital in London where they tried unsuccessfully to graft a nerve back in his arm. When the war started in 1939 he joined the British Army. When it was discovered he had fought in Spain he was discharged!

Another of the veterans present was Tom Clarke, who had served as a regular soldier for eight years till 1933. Unemployed after completing his service, he joined the Dundee Communist Party and took part in the Hunger March. He served at various fronts in Spain as a stretcher-bearer and he explained later how this came about: 'They were getting gunners, riflemen and such like, but they said: "What about stretcher bearers?" Nobody was volunteering . . . one bloke was pointing to me and says: "He'll do, he's a first-aid man."' Tom was allocated to the first aid post and to stretcher-bearing. He was later wounded – a bullet lodged in his head. A doctor, using no anaesthetic, failed to extract the bullet at a hospital he was taken to in Castellon. Eventually a dentist removed the bullet with a pair of pliers! When sent up to Tarazona, he was made a company commissar.

Arthur Nicoll was there too, a veteran of the Anti-Tank Battery which he commanded and which played such an important role at Brunete, Belchite and Teruel. Fellow veteran Hugh Sloan said of Arthur Nicoll, with whom he had taken part in political activity in Dundee during the Hunger March periods, that he 'was one of the most solidly working-class people I've ever met in my life. There was absolutely no pretensions in any way in Arthur's behaviour, either during ordinary political work in his home town, such as selling *Daily Workers*, or in Spain dealing with extraordinary incidents during battles.' When he was sent home for medical treatment after Brunete, the anti-fascist movement in the town rose to a new level. Determined to continue the fight, Arthur Nicoll returned to Spain with his younger brother.

Prestonpans Civic Centre & Park

My mate from Prestonpans was badly wounded just the day before we were surrounded and I advised him to wait on them coming up with the ambulance men that would take him down on stretchers. But he felt that the stretchers were needed for men that were more severely wounded than he was. He didn't realise how bad he was and unfortunately he died as a result of the wound. He was pumping out blood at the time. Following that, well, it was just a case of fighting and carrying on.

This is George Watters recalling the Battle of Jarama in *Voices* which recorded the impressions of many Scots who volunteered to fight fascism in Spain. He went on to describe being wounded and captured. His family thought he had been killed until, visiting a cinema, they picked him out among prisoners of war being repatriated in a Movietone newsreel. His friend from Prestonpans who died of his wound was Jock Gilmour. George Watters' brother-in-law, William Dickson, also from Prestonpans, was killed in the fighting in Brunete in July 1937.

George Watters, born in 1904, was a miner and general labourer who joined the Communist Party early in the 1920s and remained a member until his death in 1980. He describes in *Voices* how he became involved in the 1930s in the local struggles against Sir Oswald Mosley and in particular a meeting in Edinburgh's Usher Hall:

I landed down right in the second front seat . . . my job was to get up and create a disturbance right away by challenging Sir Oswald Mosley, which I did. At that time I had a pretty loud voice. . . . I was warned by William Joyce, better known later on as Lord Haw Haw, what would happen to me unless I kept quiet. There was a rush and in the rush I got a bit of a knocking about.

So it was natural when the anti-fascist war in Spain started he decided he had to go, despite being married with three children. But as he explained, 'fortunately the wife was like myself, supporting the fight of the International Brigade'.

He lived to witness his own contribution and that of his three fellow volunteers from Prestonpans honoured by a bronze memorial plaque set into the wall of the Civic Square, which was unveiled in April 1978 by International Brigade veteran, pensioners' leader and former general secretary of the TGWU, Jack Jones. A number of veterans from other parts of Scotland were also present at the memorial ceremony, along with many representatives of the local labour and trade union movement.

Local labour and trade union leaders, veterans and their supporters headed by the International Brigade banner of Scotland march in Prestonpans in April 1978 to the unveiling in the Civic Square of a bronze memorial plaque set in the wall.

Jack Jones admiring the plaque set in the wall after unveiling it. It carries the familiar line by Byron: 'They never fail who die in a great cause.'

The plaque's simple inscription reads: 'Dedicated to the memory of those who laid down their lives in the defence of democracy: Spain 1936–1939', and below, Byron is quoted: 'They never fail who die in a great cause.'

The memorial and the ceremony were organized by the Berwick and East Lothian Labour Party.

In November 1986 Prestonpans Labour Party presented a seat in the local park to commemorate the 50th anniversary of the outbreak of the anti-fascist war in Spain. The ceremony was attended by 100 people who marched from the Labour Rooms to the site of the seat, headed by a pipe band and with a silver band at the rear. Two veteran Brigaders attended the ceremony – Steve Fullarton from Glasgow, who spoke at the unveiling, and Tom Bloomfield from Kirkcaldy.

The plaque set on the seat is inscribed with the names of the four Prestonpans volunteers who fought in Spain.

A pipe band and a Fire Brigades Union banner lead Prestonpans Labour Party members, trade unionists, veterans and their friends in November 1986 to dedicate a seat with a memorial plaque to four volunteers from the town who fought in Spain.

The memorial seat presented by the Prestonpans Labour Party.

Irvine Public Library

Local heroes who died in the Spanish Civil War won't be forgotten by future generations. Cunninghame District Council has put up a plaque to commemorate John Smith from Irvine, who died 50 years ago in the Battle of Ebro. The plaque – unveiled in the Irvine Branch Library – will ensure that the memory of the International Brigade's struggle for freedom and democracy is kept alive.

The above appeared in a local newspaper in December 1988. John Smith, a widower with no children, was the only Irvine man to have volunteered and fought in Spain. According to his nephew, Peter B. Smith, of Glasgow University, his uncle was one of a family of four sons and five daughters. His father, a Glaswegian, was a sea-going engineer who later worked as an engineer in a brick works in the Irvine area. His mother, born in Irvine, was a domestic servant.

In his early teens John Smith worked at the coal face. He participated in local political life, reading the *Daily Worker* and debating with his workmates and others. He was a member of the Independent Labour Party, but like his brother later joined the Communist Party.

His decision to go to Spain to join the International Brigade came as a complete surprise to his family and friends, including the local Communist Party. Locally there was support for his action and a feeling of pride that an Irvine worker had volunteered to join the Spanish people in their fight to save their young republic. Consequently Irvine learned with shock about his death in September 1938 on the Ebro Front. He was operating as a dispatch rider, but it is not known to which units he was attached.

A cutting from a local paper of the day ran a headline: 'Irvine Man Killed in Spanish War', stating:

> Official notification has been received by Mr and Mrs Peter Smith of the death of their son, in Spain on the 8th September. Mr Smith was killed in action in the recent successful Government offensive on the Ebro front. Twenty-one months with the International Brigade Mr Smith saw service at Jarama, Pennarroya, Brunete, Belchite, Aragon and Ebro fronts. Twice wounded he was mentioned in Dispatches recently for his high courage during an enemy attack. A splendid tribute was paid to John Smith in the official telegram announcing his death.

Pennarroya was a unique, little-known engagement, where the British Battalion was more mixed internationally than in any other action.

It was the local trades council that ensured the memorial plaque to John Smith was erected on the 50th anniversary of his death. It stands in a prominent place of honour in the town library.

In Nigerhill cemetery in Irvine a family plaque to John Smith is set into one of the walls. His surviving relatives ensure flowers are laid by it each year.

CUNNINGHAME DISTRICT COUNCIL

JOHN SMITH

THIS PLAQUE COMMEMORATES THE 50TH ANNIVERSARY OF

THE DEATH OF **JOHN SMITH** OF IRVINE

A MEMBER OF THE INTERNATIONAL BRIGADE

WHO WAS KILLED ON 8TH SEPTEMBER 1938

AT THE BATTLE OF THE EBRO DURING THE SPANISH CIVIL WAR

The memorial plaque to John Smith of Irvine erected by the Cunninghame District Council in the Irvine Branch Library, Cunninghame House, Friars Cross in September 1988.

Dooega, Achill Island, Co. Mayo

Dooega

Dusk Dooega Bay; a stone
set among heathers carries Patten's name . . .

Lines from a poem by John F. Deane, writer and poet from Achill and nephew of International Brigader Peter O'Connor from Waterford for whom the poem was written.

In December 1936 'Tommy Patten fell outside Madrid one cold day. . . . His name will live on in Achill when yours and mine are forgotten.' So wrote well-known Republican fighter and author, Peadar O'Donnell, in *Salud*.

On 28 October 1984, nearly half a century after Patten was killed, O'Donnell's prophecy came true when the proud people of Dooega, Achill Island, Co. Mayo, paraded with the Dooagh Pipe Band at their head in a ceremony to unveil a magnificent stone memorial bearing the name of their heroic son and the dates 1910–1936.

On a hillock overlooking the Atlantic rollers and across from Dooega cove and his family home, the monument's simple inscription in Gaelic (which Patten spoke), Spanish and English bears witness that he 'fought bravely and died in the defence of Madrid 1936 for the Spanish Republic and all oppressed people'. Alongside the inscription the young face of Tommy Patten, etched on the dark stone, watches over the bay. The memorial was financed locally and from generous contributions from the USA.

Tommy Patten was one of the first few, far-sighted and quick to react to the fascist threat in Spain and the desperate Republican need for assistance. When journalists were announcing the fall of Madrid and that it was all over for the Republicans, the people of Madrid responded to the call 'No Pasaran!' (They Shall Not Pass!) and went in thousands to confront the fascists. Tommy Patten was one of the small number of International Brigaders who gave them moral uplift, showing they were not alone, in the desperate battles which prevented the Spanish capital falling to Franco's militarily superior forces which had advanced into the Carabanchel district in the south of the city.

He came from a family of fourteen. Like a majority of his fellow islanders, because of the impoverished conditions back home he had to seek a livelihood in Britain, where he became immersed in the Republican movement and anti-fascist groups. As he left for Spain he told his brother Owen: 'The fascist bullet that gets me, won't kill a Spanish worker.'

The memorial to Tommy Patten on the cliff top at Dooega, Achill Island, Co. Mayo, Republic of Ireland, unveiled on 28 October 1984. The inscription reads: 'In memory of Thomas Patten Dooega 1910-1936'. Then in Gaelic, Spanish and English: 'Who fought bravely and died in the defence of Madrid 1936 for the Spanish Republic and all oppressed people.'

Liberty Hall, Dublin

No better contribution could have been made by Irish trade unionists to Dublin's year as Cultural Capital of Europe in 1991 than the unveiling on Sunday 5 May of an impressive bronze memorial plaque to honour the Irish volunteers who fought in the International Brigade and gave their lives.

The plaque sculpted by Frank Maguire bears the names of those who died. The powerful relief reveals a figure lying horizontally with a gaping opening for the chest wall and abdomen. Above lies a discarded rifle and bayonet. They both merge with the tortured earth upon which they lie. The plaque is mounted on the wall of Dublin Trade Union Council's Liberty Hall at Eden Quay.

The initiative for the memorial came from Irish volunteers of the International Brigade, Alex Digges, Joe Monks and Paddy O'Daire, who had settled in the UK and had agitated for a Dublin memorial for many years.

It was realized through the organizational work of the Irish Congress of Trade Unions and Dublin Council of Trade Unions. Contributions for the plaque came from a wide cross-section of Irish people from the north and south, among them trade unionists, cabinet ministers, MPs, senators and political parties, and also from people abroad.

It was unveiled at a ceremony on the May Day weekend by the Lord Mayor of Dublin, Cllr Michael Donnelly, and was attended by trade unionists and a group of thirteen veterans of the International Brigade from Britain, Cyprus, France, Ireland, Spain and the US. The thirty-five-piece miners' orchestra, Ruhkohle Westfalen, sponsored by the German Trade Union Congress, gave a concert at Liberty Hall following the unveiling.

Dublin

Dublin Lord Mayor, Cllr Michael Donnelly, looks at the bronze memorial sculpted by Frank Maguire after unveiling it on 5 May 1991. The memorial, erected on the exterior wall of Dublin Council of Trade Unions' headquarters, Liberty Hall, Eden Quay, lists the names of Irish International Brigaders killed in Spain. Applauding is Dublin Council of Trade Unions President, Paddy Coghlan.

A close-up of the memorial.

The Irish campaign for the release from a Franco jail of their outstanding International Brigader Frank Ryan.

The President of the Dublin Council of Trade Unions, Paddy Coghlan, declared at the ceremony: 'We have deliberately set out to honour all the Irish dead, from north and south, from Ireland and the lands of our emigration, whose fight in defence of the Spanish workers is an example for today's Irish people of that unity which is our basic trade union ideal.'

Two volunteers have a special place in the history of the Irish contribution to the Spanish Republican cause: Frank Ryan, spokesman and leading figure of the Irish in the British Battalion of the International Brigade, and the young poet, Charles Donnelly.

Frank Ryan, arrested many times and imprisoned for his republican activities in Ireland, personified the best militant and revolutionary features of his people, and in Spain exhibited exceptional gifts as a leader and organizer, restoring the front in the critical days at Jarama.

He was captured at Calaceite in 1938. Ignoring the death sentence passed on him, he fearlessly challenged the brutality of the fascist jailers in Franco's prison. Despite a massive international campaign for his release, he was handed over to the Nazis and died in Dresden in 1944. In 1979 his body was taken to Dublin and re-interred as a staunch anti-fascist at a ceremony on 22 June attended by leading figures from the labour and republican movements.

Charles Donnelly, born in Dungannon, Co. Tyrone, commanded a section of the Irish in the British Battalion and was killed by an explosive bullet in the Battle of Jarama in February 1937 at the age of twenty-two. A young poet of great promise and a communist, he was imprisoned for his republican activities in Ireland, wrote a memorandum on military strategy and left unfinished a biography of James Connolly. The lines of his poem 'The Tolerance of Crows' are prophetic:

> Death comes in quantity from solved
> Problems on maps, well ordered dispositions,
> Angles of elevation and direction.

Morley's Bridge, Kilgarvan, Co. Kerry

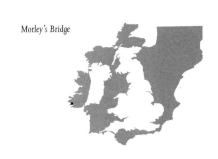

Morley's Bridge

The Spanish anti-fascist poet Rafael Alberti's epitaph for the International Brigader Michael Lehane, translated into English, explains:

> From Morley's Bridge my way I made
> A pike in my fist, fellow-workers to aid
> Death cheated in Spain, North Sea waves guard my grave
> War convoys set sail, for freedom life gave.

It is at Morley's Bridge in Kilgarvan, Co. Kerry, near his family home that you will find a simple framed memorial mounted on a stone wall amid wild flowers and ferns. In Gaelic and English it tells you Michael Lehane 'gave his young life at sea that the underprivileged of all nations would enjoy a happy and prosperous existence'.

Born in 1908 in Kilgarvan, Michael Lehane grew up on the land with a love of farming and entered an agricultural college at nineteen, but the hard, poverty-stricken life on the land forced him into the building industry in Dublin. A fellow worker described him as 'a socialist heart and soul' who could not bear to see anyone in need. He was one of the first from Ireland to join the International Brigade and had a distinguished record in Spain. Wounded in 1937, after convalescence back in Ireland he returned to Spain, crossing over the Pyrenees from France. This had to be done at night because of the French and British governments' support for so-called Non-Intervention. In the last great battle of the Ebro River in September 1938 he was wounded again just before the decision of the Republican Government that the International Brigades should withdraw.

He could not bring himself to wear a British uniform when war broke out because of the Tory Chamberlain Government's appeasement of the fascists Hitler and Mussolini in Spain. He enlisted in the Norwegian merchant navy, believing it was vital that Hitler be defeated. In 1942 he was tragically lost at sea when his ship was attacked by a German U-boat.

Michael Lehane's Republican Pay Book showing his party political affiliation as 'Anti-fascista'.

The framed memorial plaque to Michael Lehane on the stone wall at Morley's Bridge, Kilgarvan, Co. Kerry, Republic of Ireland, with its inscription in Gaelic and English.

The memorial to Michael Lehane was erected by the Killarney Republican Graves Association and unveiled at a moving ceremony in beautiful sunshine on Sunday 7 May 1989, attended by several hundred people. The unveiling was performed by his brother Pat Lehane, and wreaths were laid by his cousin Con Lehane and Timmie Joe O'Sullivan on behalf of the organizing committee. The Last Post was sounded in remembrance of Michael Lehane and his sixty-one compatriots who fell fighting in Spain.

ATGWU Hall, Waterford

Waterford

Though May Day had been traditionally celebrated by Waterford workers as elsewhere in the Republic of Ireland, in 1994 for the first time it was declared a Bank Holiday.

Members of the local Amalgamated Transport and General Workers' Union decided something special had to be done and that nothing would be more appropriate than to honour the ten Waterford heroes who fought in the British Battalion of the International Brigade in Spain nearly six decades earlier. It would also serve to expose the reactionary role played by the Christian Front, which had campaigned to support Franco Spain in 1936.

Hence with the support of the Waterford Council of Trades Unions, 1 May 1994 became a historic occasion in Waterford. Over 300 workers and their families, headed by the Waterford City Pipe Band and cheered by crowds, marched with colourful banners from Plunkett railway station, over the bridge and along the quay to the ATGWU hall in Keyser Street – the route taken fifty-six years earlier when Waterford people welcomed back Jackie Hunt, John O'Shea and Johnny Power on their return after the International Brigades were disbanded.

It was appropriate that the only surviving member of the ten Waterford International Brigaders, Peter O'Connor, who had welcomed his comrades back from Spain in 1938, should be given the honour of unveiling two exquisitely engraved plaques at the ATGWU hall at the commemorative meeting. The beautiful plaques were paid for by donations from the three branches of the ATGWU, other unions, the glass workers and the general public.

Manufactured at Waterford Crystal and designed by master engraver Tom Hayes, the glass plaques are mounted on an oak base. The left-hand plaque shows scenes from the Spanish Civil War and the one on the right bears the names of the ten heroes, headed by Maurice (Mossie) Quinlan, killed while trying to save a fellow volunteer in the battle at Jarama.

Peter O'Connor took part in the battles on the Brunete front, and his diary on 20 July 1937 records that outside the village of Villanueva del Pardillo the fascists 'made a fierce attack this morning on our right flank using 40 or 50 bombers, machine guns and tanks. Our flank gave way. We are retreating slowly. The heat is terrific. We are parched with thirst, we are now 12 hrs. without a drink. Some of our Spanish comrades have collapsed with the heat'.

Speaking at the Waterford commemorative meeting on May Day, he declared: 'The great lesson of Spain was the lesson of unity, where anti-fascists of every nation, where comrades of every religion and of none, united in a common cause to defeat Franco fascism.' He called for his compatriots to make common cause with British working people to gain 'the freedom of our country'.

The engraved glass memorial plaques manufactured at Waterford Crystal by Tom Hayes, unveiled on 1 May 1994 at the Amalgamated Transport and General Workers' Union hall in Keyser Street, Waterford.

John (Paddy) O'Shea identified by a contemporary with an 'X' on his beret.

Alexandra Gardens, Cardiff

Cardiff

The Welsh granite stone with its two memorial bronze plaques honouring Welsh International Brigaders, erected in Cardiff's Alexandra Gardens, Cathays Park, and unveiled in October 1992. The discolouring on the stone after vandals attacked the memorial with acid and fire can be seen clearly.

Fascist cowards under the anonymity of darkness set out to wipe out the history of the struggle for democracy and liberty in Cardiff in 1994.

Their objective then was the memorial to the Welsh International Brigaders erected in the city's Alexandra Gardens in Cathays Park. According to the Mid Glamorgan County Council, a concerted effort had been made by the vandals to split open the six-foot Welsh granite stone on which two bronze plaques had been attached. The culprits had used acid and fire for the purpose.

Cardiff has a history of struggle against fascism. In the thirties, Mosley's New Party and British Union of Fascists tried to get a foothold in the city, resorting to vicious anti-semitism against the sizeable Jewish minority. It was in Cardiff that the widespread South Wales campaign to aid Spain originated with the establishment in December 1936 of the Cardiff Provisional Spanish Aid Committee at a meeting of thirty-six people representing fourteen working-class organizations through the initiative of the local Communist Party.

Fortunately, the considerable work involved in successfully restoring the memorial and its two bronze plaques was undertaken by the County Council and at the time of writing everything is back in place. The stone still bears some marks, but it is hoped that with the passage of time and through weathering these will disappear.

The memorial, which stands next to the national war memorial in the beautiful ornamental gardens, featuring many cherry trees, was unveiled in October 1992 by the Lord Mayor of Cardiff, Derek Allison, in the presence of councillors, surviving Welsh Brigaders, their relatives and friends, and national representatives of the International Brigade Association. The unveiling was followed by a civic reception and buffet in the members' dining-room.

On one memorial plaque is a sculptured design representing an olive tree growing from the International Brigade emblem with a dove of peace in flight and below it the words of farewell spoken in October 1938 to the International Brigaders in Barcelona on their departure from Spain for home by Dolores Ibarruri, La Pasionaria:

'You are history. You are legend. You are the heroic example of democracy's solidarity and universality. We shall not forget you, and when the olive tree of peace puts forth its leaves again... come back!'

The plaque on the front of the memorial bears in English and Welsh the dedication to the 122 Welsh International Brigaders. Below is a quotation from philosopher Herbert Spencer: 'No one can be free till all are free.' There is another quotation, in Welsh, from the bard and pacifist T.E. Nicholas: 'Dros ryddid daear', which in English would read: 'That the earth might be free.'

The erection of the memorial was initiated by the Mid Glamorgan and South Glamorgan County Councils and Cardiff City Council. As part of a series of events to highlight the historical importance of the contribution of the International Brigade to fighting fascism in Spain, the former leader of the Labour Party, Michael Foot, gave a lecture in the Mid Glamorgan County Hall in the September before the unveiling of the memorial.

One of the most colourful characters to volunteer for Spain from South Wales was John Roberts from Aber Valley. He came to be known as 'Jack Russia' as a result of his consistent championing of the miners' cause in 1926 which led to his victimization and imprisonment. He epitomized the sacrifice, commitment and struggle of a whole generation of South Wales people. His convictions led him to Spain where he was a battalion commissar. He was badly wounded in his right shoulder from machine-gun fire on Cerro de Purburell on the Aragon front. His life story is eloquently told by his grandson Richard Felstead in *No Other Way*.

Among the speakers at the unveiling ceremony was Welsh International Brigade veteran Jim Brewer from the Rhymney Valley, who as a young man, six-foot tall and unemployed, volunteered to fight in Spain and was attached to the Anti-Tank Battery. Following his repatriation, Jim Brewer became a Labour councillor and secretary of the Welsh International Brigade Association. He described the International Brigaders as a 'unique brotherhood of people fighting despotism and defending democracy'.

In appreciation of the initiative in erecting the memorial Bill Alexander from the International Brigade Association presented the lord mayor with his definitive history of the British Battalion, *British Volunteers for Liberty*.

Close-ups of the two bronze plaques.

Miners' Library, Swansea

Swansea

Struggle inspires the highest levels of creative expression, and creative expression broadens, deepens and strengthens struggle. These are truths that were borne out in full measure by the fight against Franco fascism in Spain and in lines from a poem by the Welsh bard, T.E. Nicholas, which he called: On Remembrance of a Son of Wales who fell in Spain:

> He fell exalting brotherhood and right,
> His bleeding visage scorched by fire and smoke.

They appear in Welsh and English on the national memorial to Welshmen who served and died in Spain as volunteers with the International Brigade.

The memorial plaque made of Welsh coal, slate and steel carries a simple bilingual dedication:

> To the immortal memory of the Welshmen who with their comrades of Spain and of many nations in the ranks of the International Brigades gave their lives in support of the heroic struggle of the Spanish Republic against Fascism 1936–1939.

The Welsh national memorial plaque of Welsh coal, slate and steel in the South Wales Miners' Library at Hendrefoilan House, Swansea, listing the names of Welsh International Brigaders who fell in Spain with the inscription at the top and the verse by T.E. Nicholas below in Welsh and English. The verse reads:

He fell exalting brotherhood and right,
His bleeding visage scorched by fire and smoke.
E'en as the sweetest note is born of pain,
So shall the song of songs be born in Spain.

There follows in three columns the names of thirty-three men and where they came from, and the roll call of battles in which they fought.

Nowhere would be more appropriate than the South Wales Miners' Library at Hendrefoilan House, Gower Road, Swansea, founded in 1973, to house the Welsh national memorial.

In the Welsh coalfield there was a clearly established internationalist tradition before the anti-fascist war began in Spain. This was exemplified in the growing sympathy for the bitter struggles of Spanish miners, as illustrated in 1935 by demands to the Spanish Ambassador from the Cambrian Miners' Lodge for the release of the heroic Spanish miners and socialists held in prisons, awaiting execution, and the call in 1934 by the South Wales Miner for solidarity with the Asturian miners following their defeat, together with the declaration that the 'heroic miners of the Asturian coalfield have been fighting against the attempt to set up a Fascist government in Spain' and the appeal 'not an ounce of coal to scab on our Asturian comrades'.

The most powerful single political forum in South Wales by the mid-thirties was the Executive Council of the South Wales Miners' Federation, and given its internationalist tradition, its response to the Spanish anti-fascist war was predictable and significant. The policy of the SWMF early on in the war focused on reversing British

government policy of Non-Intervention and agitation against the Labour Party's passivity on the unequal struggle of the Spanish people.

Over half the Welshmen who fell in that war and over two-thirds of the 169 Welsh volunteers were from the mining valleys of South Wales. The SWMF provided more for the Spanish Republic in men, money and materials than any other trade union organization in the country. Its Executive Council decided in March 1937 to make a grant of £6 per week (later increased to £12 per week) to the International Brigades Dependents' Aid Fund (IBDAF) and lodges were asked to contribute a weekly sum. That year the SWMF contributed £12,500 for the Basque Children's Fund, the IBDAF, and the Spanish Medical and Milk Fund. Following the defeat of the Spanish Republican Government the SWMF sent money to Welsh volunteers imprisoned by Franco, campaigned for their release and assisted Spanish refugees arriving in Cardiff.

The SWMF's commitment was exemplified by the fact that its executive endorsed one of its leading figures, Will Paynter, to go out to Spain in 1937, when he was selected because of his political and trade union experience to look after the interests of the British Battalion at the International Brigade headquarters and to deal with individual and other problems. In Spain he gave outstanding service rallying the volunteers as political commissar at the British Battalion base. On his return he made a tremendous contribution in the service of the miners becoming in turn the president of the Welsh NUM and the national secretary of the union.

The memorial plaque in the South Wales Miners' Library was unveiled at a ceremony on 24 January 1976.

Hendrefoilan House, the South Wales Miners' Library, in its grounds at Gower Road, Swansea.

Drawings executed in Franco's prison by a Spanish Republican prisoner and addressed to Tom Jones, a miner from Wrexham (sentenced to death by Franco's henchmen, the sentence later commuted to life), who with Frank Ryan showed great fortitude during their long incarceration in prison. The legend accompanying the drawing of the the girl at the window reads: One day you will look at these pictures once again, remember that behind bars, I very willingly did them, during the hours of our shared captivity.
Always your friend
Marcelo Guerro
Bachmann
Torremolinos
(Malaga) Burgos
October 1937.

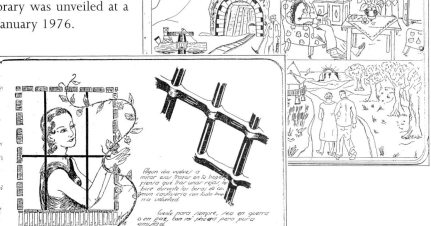

Aberdare Central Library

Aberdare

And there in the great mountain range, in a little grove of almond trees, we laid Tom Howell to rest. I said a few words of farewell but Tom is not alone there, all around him lie the graves of many Spanish and English boys.

These poignant words are from a letter to Mark Dai Jones describing how his brother Tom Howell Jones, chairman of Tower Lodge, Cynon Valley was killed by a trench mortar in an advanced position on the Sierra de Pandols mountain range near Gandesa at 2.30pm on 25 August 1938. It was written by his fellow International Brigader Edwin Greening who was an observer in the British Battalion in Spain.

The local paper the *Aberdare Leader* had a regular column where letters from volunteers to relatives and friends used to appear, showing how closely the community was bound up with the fight against fascism. The fact that it was seen in the Welsh mining valleys as being of great significance was underlined by the esteem in which the Welsh volunteers were held.

This was illustrated in 1938 when several local memorial meetings were held, arranged by a variety of organizations, as described by Hywel Francis in *Miners Against Fascism – Wales and the Spanish Civil War*. The most revealing was the Welsh National Memorial Meeting for those killed and for the returning volunteers at Mountain Ash in the December attended by over 7,000, which he described as an 'emotion-charged evening' encapsulating the broad support for the Aid Spain movement in Wales over the previous two years. Paul Robeson sang, recited and spoke at that meeting, saying: 'I am here because I know that these fellows fought not only for Spain but for me and the whole world. I feel it is my duty to be here.' The Dean of Chichester, a Welshman, said the International Brigaders had given their lives for something of eternal value.

Among the audience of people from the surrounding valleys were Italians, English and 100 people from Cardiff's West Indian community and pride of place was given to the relatives of those killed in Spain, to the clenched-fisted Basque children and the thirty of the seventy Welsh volunteers who had been repatriated from Spain.

Nearly thirty years later the Aberdare Labour Party and the trades council raised funds locally from various organizations, the miners prominent among them, for a memorial to the volunteers who fought in Spain.

The memorial in the form of a wooden-framed sculptured relief showing a star with the words 'No Pasaran!' underneath and heads on one side with a fallen volunteer at the bottom, was erected in the Aberdare Labour rooms on 16 December 1967.

Its legend proclaims that it is a 'Tribute to all those who served and died with the International Brigade during the Spanish Civil War 1936–39', naming among them seven from the Aberdare constituency, two of whom died on 25 August 1938 – William Burston and Tom Howell Jones.

Another unveiling by the former Labour leader Michael Foot took place in June 1986, after the plaque was transferred from the Labour Party rooms, which were being sold, and installed in the foyer of the Aberdare Central Library, where it is to be found today.

At that memorial event two of the Cynon valley survivors were present – Will Lloyd and Morien Morgan. Morien Morgan, who was taken prisoner in Spain, had played a major role in organizing this and other commemoration events by the Cynon Valley CLP and its affiliated organizations, the Co-operative Party and Society, youth and women's sections.

The relief carvings in wood forming the memorial installed in the foyer of the Aberdare Central Library, unveiled in June 1986.

Rhondda Borough Council Chamber

Rhondda

In 1989, from 30 August, the Rhondda held a unique week of activities: 'Rhondda Remembers 1939–1945', which included an Evacuees' Weekend when all the children evacuated there in 1939–40 to escape the bombs of Hitler's blitz were invited back to the Rhondda to remember.

The Rhondda Borough Council convened a special council meeting at Pentre on Saturday 2 September, when a resolution was adopted with acclamation, which paid tribute to the 'brave and valiant' men who fought in the British Battalion of the International Brigade and expressed thanks and sympathy to their families.

At the conclusion of the special council meeting a striking memorial plaque bearing the names of seven Rhondda men who gave their lives in Spain and twenty-four who fought and returned from Spain was unveiled by Jack Jones, an International Brigader, pensioners' leader and former general secretary of the Transport and General Workers' Union.

The memorial plaque in the Rhondda Council building, Pentre, unveiled on 2 September 1989.

THIS MEMORIAL HONOURS THE MEN FROM THE RHONDDA
WHO FOUGHT IN THE INTERNATIONAL BRIGADE WITH THE SPANISH PEOPLE
IN DEFENCE OF DEMOCRACY AND PEACE 1936–1939

SEVEN REST IN THE SOIL OF SPAIN

Alec Cummings	Tonypandy
William J. Davies	Penygraig
Harry Dobson	Blaenclydach
Sydney James	Treherbert
David J. Jones	Llwynypia
Frank Owen	Maerdy
Thomas Picton	Treherbert

TWENTY FOUR RETURNED TO CONTINUE THEIR STRUGGLE

Tom Adlam	Ystrad	A. Lewis	Rhondda
George Baker	Gelli	Hector Manning	Dinas
Will Beavan	Penygraig	Frank Middleton	Trealaw
Archie Cook	Ystrad	Alfred J. Morris	Maerdy
D. D. Davies	Gelli	William Paynter	Cymmar
T. E. S. Davies	Penygraig	G. Poustie	Treorchy
W. J. Foulkes	Treherbert	Edward Powell	Treorchy
William J. Griffiths	Llwynypia	William Price	Ton Pentre
D. M. Jones	Maerdy	J. Roberts	Trealaw
Emrys Jones	Clydach Vale	Jack Roberts	Tonypandy
Jack Jones	Blaenclydach	Arthur Williams	Penygraig
Tom Jones	Penygraig	Alun M. Williams	Gilfach

ERECTED BY THE RHONDDA BOROUGH COUNCIL
AND
UNVEILED BY MR. JACK JONES, C.H., M.B.E., F.C.I.T.
former General Secretary of the Transport and General Workers' Union
who fought in the International Brigade

2ND SEPTEMBER 1989

Two of the twenty-four, Tom Adlam and Archie Cook, survived to witness on that day the esteem in which they were held in the valleys. A procession from the council chamber to St Peter's Church for a remembrance service was led by the mayor and councillors in their robes and followed by all the voluntary organizations of the valleys, Scouts, Guides, the Salvation Army, several hundred returned evacuees and their hosts. Archie Cook was too frail to march, but Tom Adlam carried the battered International Brigade banner with its roll-call of battles, to cheers from bystanders.

The Rhondda was in the forefront of activity to help the Spanish people. Sometimes a bell borrowed from school would be rung along the streets to assist in the collection of 'Food for Spain' as men and women collected gifts in a pram or a pushcart. Everyone in the valleys was involved, the churches, the miners' lodges, the clubs and choirs and all political parties.

On the Roll of Honour in the Rhondda Council Chamber, among the names of those who gave their lives in Spain is that of Harry Dobson, an unemployed Rhondda miner, who was imprisoned for three months for fighting Mosley's Blackshirts and whose first words on being released were: 'How do I get to Spain?' Political commissar to the Major Attlee Company, he distinguished himself during the battles around Aragon when he and his comrades bluffed their way through the fascist lines to the Republican forces after escaping from their captors.

Harry Dobson described the breakthrough as follows: 'We held a council of war, decided where to break through and the tactics to adopt. After a short but fierce struggle at close quarters we broke through. A few hours later we reached the Ebro . . . Now we are back [with the British Battalion] and looking forward eagerly to retracing our steps and meeting the Fascists on more equal terms.'

His wish was realized when the Republican forces triumphantly swept back across the Ebro. Harry Dobson, who had survived the sinking by a Nazi torpedo of the ship *City of Barcelona* which was taking him and fellow volunteers to Spain and had fought in nearly every battle in Spain, fell to the fascists in the last battle of the British Battalion.

Another name on the Roll of Honour is that of Jack Jones, a Rhondda miner, who was captured in March 1938 at Calaceite. Within four days of capture, Jack Jones with other leading communists began to organize to give political leadership to their fellow prisoners in the military prison of Zaragoza.

Harry Dobson, who bluffed his way through enemy lines to rejoin the Republican forces on the Aragon front.

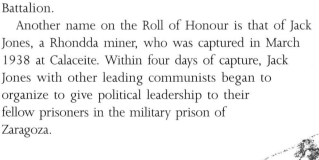

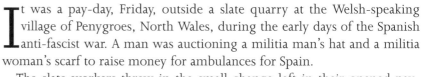

Penygroes

It was a pay-day, Friday, outside a slate quarry at the Welsh-speaking village of Penygroes, North Wales, during the early days of the Spanish anti-fascist war. A man was auctioning a militia man's hat and a militia woman's scarf to raise money for ambulances for Spain.

The slate workers threw in the small change left in their opened pay-packets, but later the auctioneer to his surprise discovered two unopened packets which both moved and worried him because the workers' pay was so pitifully small. It was all the more remarkable because the area was noted for its Lloyd George liberal rather than socialist traditions.

The auctioneer was anti-fascist Douglas Hyde who had made several trips to raise money for the ambulance fund in villages and towns in mid- and north Wales. When he arrived in Penygroes he had been advised to go to the quarry to publicize a fund-raising meeting and the showing of Ivor Montagu's documentary film *Defence of Madrid* in the village hall that evening.

That visit resulted in one young unemployed man from the village, George Fretwell, leaving for Spain – he did not tell his family where he was going, just asked his brother to look after his bicycle and disappeared. He wrote home from Paris and later from Plaza del Fargo, Spain. Nothing more was heard from him.

Photograph of young George Fretwell taken before he set off for Spain, from the family scrapbook in the possession of his brother Dafydd.

George was an ardent member of the Territorials with the rank of sergeant. He was one of three sons and a daughter. His father had had both his legs amputated in the First World War and his mother had a hard time bringing up the children on a small army pension.

Two months later on 12 February 1937 George was killed, aged twenty-six, in the bloody battle for Arganda Bridge, in the Jarama Valley, a crucial engagement to prevent the Franco forces cutting the road between Madrid and Valencia. He went into battle at 7 a.m. with over 600 members of the British Battalion; 12 hours later, less than 150 answered the roll-call. He was buried the next day with thirty other International Brigade volunteers in an olive grove.

Bill Rust in his book *Britons in Spain* explained how the badly armed volunteers, most of them facing their baptism of fire 'steadily held their positions for hour after hour, under a broiling sun while death rained down on them. To retreat, to run away would have been easy. But these men had left their homes to fight Fascism, and the order of the day was "hold out at all costs". They held out and helped to hold the enemy off. During these February days, the 12th, 13th and 14th, the Republican forces in the Arganda–Morata sector resisted the heaviest attacks of the entire battle of Jarama, and succeeded in bringing the fascist advance to a halt.' Madrid was consequently saved from fascism for another two years.

It was only in the following year, 1938, that his family was told George was 'missing, believed killed'. But not until 1970 did they know precisely how and where he was killed, through fellow Welsh veteran International Brigader Glyn Evans, who had been with George in Spain. The following year as a result of a newspaper article about George, another veteran, George Magee of Cheshire, visited the family and told them he had been in the burial party.

When in 1938 the news of his death reached Penygroes the small village community was divided – some saw him as a hero and were proud that he had gone from their little community and died for Spain, but others, shocked by his death, were resentful that a young life had been thrown away.

Much time has passed to heal the wound and what in particular united the small community was the decision to launch an appeal fund for a memorial in Penygroes for George Fretwell – the idea came from people who had grown up with George and was discussed over a number of years by the Memorial Hall Committee. Eventually a sum of £207 was raised and the committee decided that a memorial in the form of a slate tablet and a slate clock be purchased.

On 7 January 1991 at a ceremony attended by over fifty people, including his brother Dafydd, the plaque was unveiled in the Memorial Hall. It carries the following inscription in Welsh: 'In memory of George Ernest Fretwell who lost his life whilst fighting with the International Brigade in the Spanish Civil War 1936–1939 at Jarama Valley 12th February 1937.'

Dafydd Fretwell (right) at the unveiling of the plaque to his brother, George.

The memorial plaque to George Fretwell.

Newcastle City Hall & Tyne and Wear Trades Council

Newcastle upon Tyne

There was a powerful tradition in Tyne and Wear, of fighting fascist intimidation, defending sections of the labour movement against fascist attacks and driving fascists off the streets. The Newcastle daily, *The Journal*, in May 1934 reported: 'Within the past three months Newcastle has achieved the unfortunate distinction of becoming one of the storm centres of aggressive Fascism in Great Britain. . . . Since 1 April of this year there have been no less than 14 street fights in Newcastle and Gateshead.'

It is against this background that the movement for solidarity with the young Spanish Republic sprung into being. At least fifty men and women from the area of Tyne and Wear and County Durham served with the International Brigade and some forty more from Cleveland and Northumberland. More than half of them were killed and most of the others were wounded at least once.

The local paper described a memorial meeting on Sunday 15 January 1939 at the City Hall, Newcastle: 'The balcony of the hall was draped with Spanish colours. Suspended from the ceiling and reaching down to the stage were two giant scrolls of red silk. Inscribed upon them in silver lettering were the names and home towns of 25 men of Durham and Northumberland: "They Died for Democracy and Us".' The paper, probably *The Wearsider*, said that according to its reporter the memorial meeting that night provided one of the most stirring occasions he had known.

The meeting was opened by a well-known radical, the former Newcastle upon Tyne Labour MP and Lord Lieutenant of Northumberland, Sir Charles Trevelyan, who said: 'These men had had the foresight to see that an attack on the liberty of the Spanish people was a blow against democracy. They had realised that a happy people must be a free people. Theirs had been a foresight such as is denied to the darkened souls of our present Government leaders.' The Newcastle Co-operative Women's Choir sang 'Jerusalem' and the Spanish national anthem, 'Himno de Riego', as the audience of 2,000 rose to their feet. Down the centre aisles came members of the International Brigade led by standard bearers and a tremendous ovation was accorded them. Chopin's 'Funeral March' was played, followed by the Last Post being sounded as the audience stood in silence.

Isobel Brown made a stirring appeal for aid for the memorial fund of the International Brigade and donations from miners' lodges were handed in from all parts of the hall – a total collection of £142 13s 6d was handed in with donations coming also from the Labour, Co-operative, Communist and *Tribune* sections in the audience, the paper reported.

In July 1986 the Newcastle upon Tyne City Council asked local veteran International Brigader Frank Graham to plant a tree in the grounds of the Civic Centre to mark the 50th anniversary of the start of the anti-fascist war in Spain. Present at the tree-planting ceremony were another veteran volunteer, John Henderson, Lord Mayor Peter Laing, Leader of the Council Jeremy Beeching, trade union representatives and Mr Robert Craig from the Spanish consulate in Newcastle. Later the tree was replaced by another, a London plane tree which is native to the Mediterranean.

In March 1989 the County Association of Trades Councils and Newcastle City Council both laid plaques to pay formal tribute to the volunteers from the area. The City Council plaque noted that the tree had been planted to 'commemorate the 50th anniversary of the Spanish Civil War'. The plaque from the County Association said that it was to 'commemorate those men from the Tyne and Wear region who died fighting fascism in Spain 1936–1939'. Present at the ceremony were veteran volunteers Frank Graham and Tommy Kerr (who ran away at

International Brigade veteran Frank Graham about to place decorative plants at the memorial tree in the grounds of Newcastle upon Tyne Civic Centre, with former Lord Mayor Peter Laing and Newcastle Trades Council secretary Alec McFadden, in March 1986.

sixteen to fight Franco), Jeremy Beeching and Peter Laing, trade union leader Alec McFadden and MPs Jim Cousins and David Clelland.

While the City Council's metal plaque remains firmly in place on its concrete base by the tree, regrettably vandals have more than once pulled out of the ground the trade union plaque which stood on a stainless steel spike. At the time of writing the city authorities were in the process of restoring the plaque to its site and concreting it into the ground.

Frank Graham, who distinguished himself in Spain and was wounded in the stomach and spine, like many other volunteers had to cross into Spain over the Pyrenees in darkness – he had survived with fellow volunteers when his ferry was torpedoed by a Nazi submarine in the Mediterranean, while Will Lower from Sunderland drowned. Frank Graham described his experience in the historic Battle of Jarama:

> Before we had retreated far with the Moors barely 200 yards behind, several machine guns opened up on our right. The Moors were mowed down in scores. It was our machine gun company which was in action for the first time. . . . Seeing the rest of the Battalion in full retreat the Moors thought the battle was over. They had a rude awakening.

Two Tyne and Wear women served with the medical unit of the British Battalion: Winifred Wilson, a hospital nurse from Gosforth who was with the original contingent that set out in 1936, and Enid Ramshaw, a district nurse from Whickham who served on the front for the final six months of the Ebro campaign. They nursed at field dressing-stations under fire, evacuated patients from a base hospital into a railway tunnel during an air raid and had to work under appalling conditions and with minimal equipment.

The City Council plaque.

Bob Elliott House, Blyth

The elderly residents of thirty specially designed flats in a sheltered block in Blyth Valley, Tyne and Wear, had a pleasant surprise at the end of August 1986 when they were all presented with a bottle of wine and a copy of the International Brigade memorial brochure *In Defence of Liberty* by British Battalion veteran Frank Graham of Newcastle, on behalf of the International Brigade Association.

It was a gesture by the IBA to acknowledge and welcome the fact that in May that year the Borough of Blyth Valley had named the sheltered accommodation in Wright Street as Bob Elliott House, to honour the International Brigader who died from wounds he received fighting with the British Battalion when it routed the fascist forces at Villanueva on the Brunete front in July 1937.

A joint working party from the council's housing department, the health authority and social services department had met three years earlier to consider the design of the building so that the needs of the more frail and disabled elderly could be catered for.

Bob Elliott House was opened by Borough of Blyth Valley Mayor, Derek Raffle. Present at the official opening were Bob Elliott's only surviving sister, 89-year-old Mrs Margaret Milburn and her two sons, Thomas and John. Mrs Milburn was very moved and said she felt proud: 'It's marvellous that Bob has been remembered after all these years.'

Blyth

Residents of Bob Elliott House sitting in front of the memorial name plaque.

Bob Elliott was an unemployed miner and prominent member of the National Unemployed Workers' Movement. His advice and practical assistance before the Courts of Referees and Public Assistance Committee were highly esteemed. In 1931 he was elected for the Croft ward as a communist to the Blyth Council and re-elected in 1937 because of the staunch service he gave. In Spain he fulfilled the important responsibility of a company political commissar and was described as a stern disciplinarian.

Like a number of Brigaders, Bob Elliott kept a diary in Spain. Here are some extracts written during the Battle of Jarama:

Tuesday, February 16th. I go with seven other volunteers to hold an advance post. Wednesday, February 17th. The night is cold and disagreeable. Some Spaniards arrive with a machine gun to repair but it is not possible. We rest in an advanced position all night. The Dimitrov Battalion is very well organized. They sing while shooting at the enemy. Friday, February 19th. Again in the front line. Food is infinitely better. The Moors are howling as though they were in hell. We opened fire on them . . . peace. Then a great aerial battle. Saturday, February 20th. It is bitterly cold. Some new comrades have arrived. We advance half a kilometre. We dig in until midnight. Nothing of importance until a shell explodes near us. Cunningham's helmet is blown off. A good comrade and his mate are wounded, one of them with his foot blown off.

Bob Elliott House in Blyth Valley, Tyne and Wear.

Town Hall, Middlesbrough

There is an extraordinary story attached to the memorial plaque to the Teesside International Brigaders which today is to be found in the Middlesbrough Town Hall.

It begins in 1939 when Teesside volunteers held a gathering in Stockton with friends to honour their comrades who had fallen on Spanish soil fighting for liberty. Around a hundred men from north-east England volunteered to go to Spain: over twenty-five did not return, ten of whom were from Teesside.

At that gathering they all pledged to continue the fight against fascism and to extend solidarity to those fighting against the Nazis and Italian fascists. The gathering also decided a permanent memorial to the Brigaders should be made in the form of a plaque.

Harold W. Bennet, a carpenter and french polisher from Kent, who was visiting relatives and was present at the gathering, asked that he be permitted to make the plaque as his final piece of work as he was losing his sight. A week after making the plaque he went blind. He handed the plaque to an International Brigader, Tommy Chivers, to do the gold lettering.

The wooden memorial plaque with its gold lettering unveiled in 1992 in the Council Chamber of Middlesbrough Town Hall. The inscription reads: To Defend Liberty . . . they typified the real Britons hatred of the tyrant; they went to safeguard peace and the arts of peace, that humanity might go forward. They went to help the defenceless Spanish people fight the invading armies. They went to save their loved ones, and us from the horrors of fascism. Because they loved peace, they went out to fight . . . from Tees-side.

Dave Goodman.

John Longstaff.

The plaque was kept in a private house, but was apparently stolen in the 1960s. Miraculously it was found in 1983 by a school teacher in a junk yard in Acton, West London. She bought it and handed it to the International Brigade Association for it to be returned to Teesside.

John Longstaff, who at the age of fifteen marched to London in 1934 along with the Stockton unemployed to demand jobs, was among the youngest to volunteer for Spain when he went out there at the age of seventeen. It was his initiative which resulted in Sir Maurice Sutherland, chairman of the Cleveland County Council, arranging for the plaque to be placed in the Council Chambers in Middlesbrough Town Hall.

At the ceremony in 1992 to unveil it many British Battalion veterans and their relatives were present as well as the mayors of Hartlepool, Middlesbrough, Stockton and Redcar, and councillors and trade unionists from all areas of Cleveland. Many well-attended and representative annual memorial gatherings have been held since then.

The beautiful plaque, now fully restored, bears the names of the ten heroes who died in the fight 'To Defend Liberty' and lists the battles where they fell 'to safeguard peace and the arts of peace, that humanity might go forward'.

Dave Goodman, captured and imprisoned in Franco's gaols, was a son of a small Middlesbrough trader. He vividly illustrates in his story, *From the Tees to the Ebro: My Road to Spain*, the political and economic background obtaining on Teesside in the thirties that moulded the political outlook of men like him: 'Of all the issues with which we were concerned in 1937 the war in Spain was the one which stirred the deepest emotions. It became daily more clear that on Spanish soil and, overwhelmingly, with Spanish lives a decisive battle was being fought which would determine whether fascism – especially Hitler's Nazi variety – would be halted or continue to threaten the peace of the world.'

As in other parts of the country, the collection of funds and food for Spain was a regular part of political activity on Teesside. Twenty-two Basque children were billeted with families in the Teesside area where the Basque Children's Committee, affiliated to the National Joint Committee for Spanish Relief carried out great work in looking after the refugee children for over two years and organizing such fund raising activities as the Spanish Christmas Appeal for providing suitable winter clothing and Christmas gifts.

Collecting-sheets from those days show that despite the unemployment, poverty and hardship they were experiencing themselves, people gave anything from threepence to two shillings.

Trade Union Centre, Liverpool

> The rifles you will never hold again
> In other hands still speak against the night

Liverpool

This moving extract comes from the memorial plaque to the twenty-seven Merseyside volunteers who fought and died in the ranks of the International Brigade.

One of those who returned from Spain, literally came back from the dead. His family had received a death certificate stating that he had been killed on 3 May 1938. He was seaman Jack Coward, who later told his story in a booklet *Back from the Dead* published by the *Daily Worker*.

It is the story of a man who survived because he was endowed with an unbreakable conviction, incredible courage, determination and ingenuity, and almost limitless physical endurance.

An appeal had been sent for volunteers to serve in the Republican navy. Jack Coward was one of the five to go from Merseyside. He had served as a boatswain in the Royal Navy and fulfilled a similar function in the Republican torpedo boats for a year, and then decided he wanted to get to grips directly with the enemy and left to join the British Battalion.

He was commanding No. 4 Company when he was ambushed at Calaceite – he managed to escape to the hills to join up with guerrillas. Captured, he escaped and linked up with a group of peasants. He was caught and escaped again to rejoin his peasant friends. Unfortunately, being behind enemy lines they were bombed by Republican planes and as a result of the blast shock Jack Coward became deaf, lost his voice temporarily and his hair turned white. He was caught again, but was not identified as an International Brigader, having disguised himself as a poor peasant. He was sent to the San Pedro concentration camp where 6,000 Spanish civilians were interned, but kept apart from the International Brigade prisoners. Jack Coward still managed to escape identification explaining away his deafness by saying it had happened when a boiler on a ship he was working on exploded. At the end of the war some prisoners over forty-five years of age were released. With his white hair he had the appearance of an older man and so he was able to make his way to Vigo on the north-west coast and to stow away on a British ship by pretending to be a drunken British sailor. He hid in the coal bunkers until the ship reached Gibraltar, and finally made it back to Liverpool to be hailed by his colleagues in the dockers' union branch as 'the best news for many months'.

The cover of the pamphlet by Jack Coward in which he described his experiences in Spain. It was published by the Daily Worker.

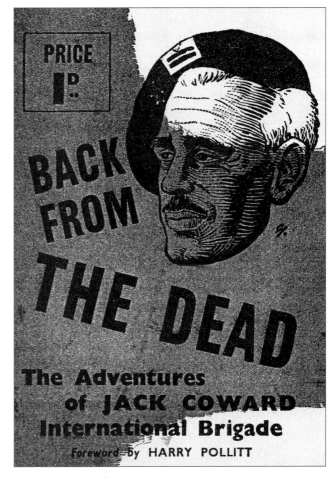

TO THE MERSEYSIDE MEN OF
THE INTERNATIONAL BRIGADES
WHO FELL IN THE STRUGGLE
FOR DEMOCRACY IN SPAIN

R. BEADLES FEB. 1937. JARAMA.
W. BOGLE FEB. 1937. JARAMA.
G. HARRIS JULY 1937. BRUNETE.
E. JACKMAN FEB. 1937. JARAMA.
R. KIRK FEB. 1937. JARAMA.
G. MCEWEN FEB. 1937. JARAMA.
T. MCLEOD FEB. 1937. JARAMA.
J. T. NORBURY FEB. 1937. JARAMA.
T. O'BRIEN FEB. 1937. JARAMA.
F. PROCTOR AUG. 1938. EBRO.
J. REDMOND MARCH 1938. ARAGON.
W. SMITH MARCH 1938. ARAGON.
L. TANKLEVITCH JULY 1938. EBRO.

L. BIBBY FEB. 1937. JARAMA.
W. J. GILES FEB. 1937. JARAMA.
G. HOLLANBY APR. 1938. GANDESA
F. KILLICK FEB. 1937. JARAMA.
A. MCCABE AUG. 1937. QUINTO.
G. MCKEOWN JUNE 1937. JARAMA.
J. NEWMAN FEB. 1937. JARAMA.
F. NORTON FEB. 1937. JARAMA.
J. D. OWENS FEB. 1937. JARAMA.
J. PETERSON APR. 1938. GANDESA.
T. SILCOCK FEB. 1937. JARAMA.
J. STEWART FEB. 1937. JARAMA.
J. WALSH FEB. 1937. JARAMA.

G. WESTFIELD OCT. 1937. ARAGON.

THE RIFLES YOU WILL NEVER HOLD AGAIN
IN OTHER HANDS STILL SPEAK AGAINST THE NIGHT.
BROTHERS HAVE FILLED YOUR PLACES IN THE RANKS
WHO WILL REMEMBER HOW YOU DIED FOR RIGHT.
THE DAY YOU TOOK THOSE RIFLES UP. DEFIED
THE POWER OF AGES. AND VICTORIOUS DIED.

COMRADES, SLEEP NOW. FOR ALL YOU LOVED SHALL BE.
YOU DID NOT SEEK FOR DEATH. BUT FINDING IT -
AND SUCH A DEATH - BETTER THAN SHAMEFUL LIFE.
REST NOW CONTENT. A FLAME OF HOPE IS LIT.
THE FLAG OF FREEDOM FLOATS AGAIN UNFURLED
AND ALL YOU LOVED LIVES RICHLIER IN THE WORLD.

LON ELLIOT.

THIS PLAQUE WAS DONATED
BY MERSEYSIDE COUNTY COUNCIL.
AND UNVEILED ON 16TH NOVEMBER 1985
BY COUNTY COUNCILLOR EDITH LAWRENSON AND
J. L. JONES. INTERNATIONAL BRIGADE ASSOCIATION

*The memorial plaque to the Merseyside men of the
International Brigade unveiled on 16 November
1985 at the Trade Union, Community and
Unemployed Resource Centre.*

He had been subjected to torture and beaten senseless on more than one occasion when in Spain. Once when he was hiding in bushes by a farm a group of Franco's Moorish soldiers arrived. Seeing the Moorish sergeant dragging off a young girl to rape her, he dashed out from the bushes and grabbed the sergeant by the throat, only to have a rifle butt smashed on his head, knocking him unconscious.

During the Second World War Jack Coward trained units of the Palestine navy in gunnery. He died aged sixty-five from a heart attack in October 1971, when a memorial meeting was held for him in Liverpool.

Another Merseysider, Frank Deegan returned from Spain and eventually set down in his book, *There's No Other Way*, his experiences of being in and out of work, of strikes and involvement with the unemployed workers movement in the 1930s. He described being beaten up by Mosley's fascists in Liverpool, then the fighting with the British Battalion in Spain, and the struggles he returned to in the Merseyside area when he went to work in the docks as an honoured member of the TGWU.

Former general secretary of the TGWU, Moss Evans, in a foreword to Frank Deegan's book, concluded that: 'his history is that of many thousands of others. It is partisan and proudly so. It is honest and of a time when to tell the truth was a revolutionary act.'

Frank Deegan was an honoured guest at Merseyside's tribute to the International Brigade in November 1985 when the memorial plaque was unveiled at the Trade Union, Community and Unemployed Resource Centre by Merseyside County Council chairwoman Mrs E. Lawrenson. One of the speakers at that historic occasion was Major José Antonio Valledor, former commander of the 15th International Brigade.

Merseyside Left Theatre gave performances of works first staged in 1937 as part of the struggle against Franco and international fascism. The Bacchus and Vauxy Theatre performed songs of the labour movement.

Merseyside International Brigaders return home from Spain.

Town Hall, Manchester

Manchester

George Brown.

Lancashire in the thirties was grim. Unemployment was rife, housing conditions were generally poor, education was attenuated and higher education virtually unknown. Yet through this gloom gleamed a light that has continued illuminating the political scene ever since, showing the way to progress, change and hope for the future. The International Brigade in Spain was the spearhead in this country of the anti-fascist force that defeated Hitler in 1945. Those who lost their lives in Spain were the first of many; those who returned continued the struggle on all fronts . . .

This eloquent background comment by Edmund and Ruth Frow is in a pamphlet dedicated to *Greater Manchester Men Who Fought in Spain*. It was published in connection with the unveiling in February 1983, on the 46th anniversary of the Battle of Jarama, of a memorial to them at Manchester Town Hall, by Deputy Lord Mayor Hugh Lee. It proved to be one of the biggest reunions in Britain of International Brigaders and their supporters since the end of the Spanish anti-fascist war.

The Town Hall was an appropriate place for such a memorial as adjacent is the site of the 1819 Peterloo massacre when the cavalry charged a peaceful demonstration for reform, killing 11 people and leaving nearly 500 injured.

The memorial, an exceptionally fine wood carving surrounded by brass and slate, is by local working-class sculptor Sol Garson. It has as its centre-piece the International Brigade emblem being held up by two hands and, below, the moving words of farewell to the International Brigaders from La Pasionaria in Barcelona on their departure from Spain. The dove of peace, flying off, crowns the whole memorial.

The Manchester branch of the Society of Graphical and Allied Trades (SOGAT) played an extremely generous role in assisting in the realization of the memorial, commissioned by the Greater Manchester International Brigade Association.

The contribution of the North West to anti-fascist war in Spain was considerable: about 130 went from the Greater Manchester area, of whom at least 35 were killed, with over one-third being killed during the Battle of Jarama. The volunteers, as from other areas, represented many facets of life in the mid-thirties; some were unemployed, some had good jobs, many were active in the anti-fascist campaigns. Many were outdoor enthusiasts, ramblers and campers, including veterans of the historic mass trespass on Kinder Scout in 1932 to protest at closure of open land by landowners.

One of those from Manchester who lost their lives in Spain was the city organizer of the Communist Party, member of its national executive committee and one of the company political commissars of the British Battalion, George Brown. He was a political figure of great stature who won the respect of both political allies and foes for his leadership in the campaigns of the unemployed and in defence of workers' rights.

George Brown was killed in 1937 in the battle for Brunete, which cost the British Battalion 300 men – he was shot by the fascists as he lay

The carved wood memorial in Manchester Town Hall
made by Sol Garson and unveiled by Deputy Lord Mayor
Hugh Lee on 12 February 1983, which has inscribed
on it the speech of La Pasionaria bidding farewell to the
International Brigaders in Barcelona.

Maurice Levine with a comrade-in-arms.

wounded by the roadside. His death brought a deep sense of loss to the whole of the Manchester community – several memorial events were held in his honour in the months and years that followed.

Maurice Levine, whose parents were Lithuanian Jewish immigrants who had eleven children, was a cutter in the clothing business. He worked in Australia for a while, and on returning to England in 1931 joined the Communist Party. He was one of the ramblers who took part in the Kinder Scout trespass and anti-fascist activity in Manchester. In *Cheetham to Cordova* he tells his life story, including his experiences in Spain where he was wounded twice, the first time by young Republican soldiers when he was returning from enemy lines after a night raid. He saw service in the Royal Army Service Corps towards the end of the Second World War and in Normandy was made a regimental policeman for his unit. In July 1986 he joined other veterans like Syd Booth, Alex Ferguson and Ben Goodman when they were given a civic reception.

Sam Wild, a labourer who had served in the British navy as a boatswain's mate, was wounded on several occasions in Spain, returning after each period in hospital to resume service at the front. Through his intrepid fearlessness under fire he became one of the last commanders of the British Battalion, during the crucial battle at Teruel. In *British Volunteers for Liberty*, the author Bill Alexander writes that Sam Wild showed 'courageous and undaunted leadership', for which he was more than once promoted in the field.

While the British Battalion was waiting to be repatriated, Sam Wild declared: 'The British Battalion is prepared to carry on the work begun here to see to it that our 500 comrades who sleep for ever beneath Spanish soil shall serve as an example to the entire British people in the struggle against fascism.' Sam Wild lived up to his word on his return.

Sam Wild, the last commander of the British Battalion, with American doctor on his right and Spanish company commander Cipriano on his left.

On 1 May 1937 at a memorial meeting in Manchester for 'Dare Devil' dirt-track rider Clem Beckett, who had been killed in the February at Arganda Bridge, his widow Leda said that he, 'like hundreds of other brave men, went to Spain not because he was reckless of his life, or because he wanted adventure, or, as the *Daily Mail* suggested, because he was ready to sell his life for £6 a week – he went to Spain to face death because he loved life.'

Oldham

Pamphlet to honour Oldham's hero killed in Spain, published by the local Dependants' Committee.

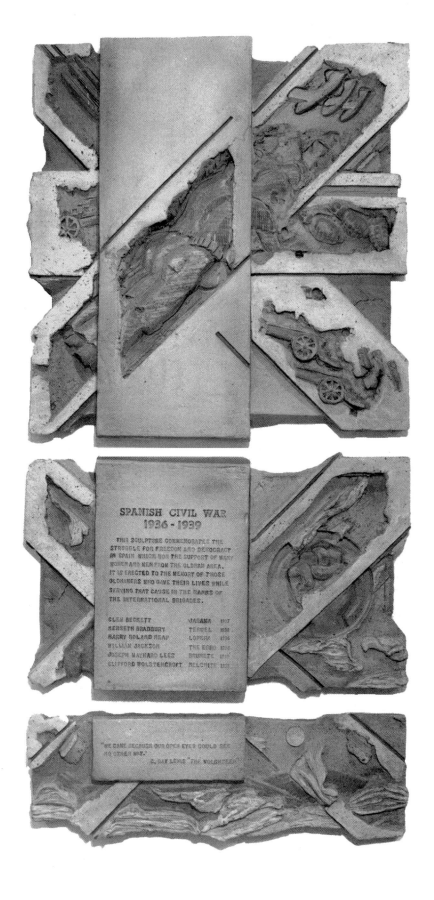

The memorial sculpted in 1980 by John Fordham
and erected in the entrance hall of Oldham
Museum.

Visitors to Oldham Museum will find a permanent memorial to Clem Beckett and his fellow volunteers in the form of an original and beautifully designed relief sculpture in the entrance hall. The memorial was commissioned from sculptor John Fordham by the museum in 1980. The inscription on it reads:

> Spanish Civil War 1936–1939 This sculpture commemorates the struggle for freedom and democracy in Spain which won the support of many women and men from the Oldham area. It is erected to the memory of those Oldhamers who gave their lives while serving that cause in the ranks of the International Brigades.

There follow the names of Clem Beckett and five of his fellow volunteers with the dates and places of their deaths in Spain.

Also on display are the photographs of the six who died and of four other volunteers who returned to carry on the struggle for peace. These photographs appeared originally on the cover of a folder, *The Oldham Men who Fought in Spain 1936–1938*, published in 1986 by the Oldham Museum (then known as the Oldham Local Interest Centre) as part of a 50th anniversary memorial exhibition held from January to May that year. The memorial folder explained the history of the International Brigades and gave a short biography of each of the ten volunteers.

The museum also has a copy of *Songs of the Spanish Civil War*, dedicated to the Oldham men who fought in Spain and published in February 1986, and pamphlets about Clem Beckett and his fellow volunteers.

Clement Henry Beckett was a very colourful personality – though a keen rugby player, he was known for his unquenchable passion for motorbikes. He became one of the nation's most brilliant riders seen on the track in the early days of speedway. His exploits on the track earned him the nickname 'Dare Devil'. One year, he appeared at Coventry, Manchester and Rochdale tracks all in one day, breaking records at each. He founded the Dirt Track Riders' Association to protect the interests of riders, was a member of the Blacksmiths' Union and joined the Young Communist League in 1924.

He was one of the first Lancashire men to volunteer for Spain where he served as a mechanic, ambulance driver and expert machine-gunner. He was a close friend of writer Christopher Caudwell. They were both killed as they were covering the British Battalion's retreat with a Chatto machine-gun at Arganda Bridge, in the battle to keep the Madrid–Valencia road open.

After his death a fellow volunteer wrote to Leda Beckett: 'He had nerves of steel and his conduct was an inspiration to all of us. I had to write this letter to you, for Clem was one of the finest men – in every respect – that I ever met.'

Town Hall, St Helens

St Helens

The cover of the commemorative pamphlet about Bill Feeley produced as a tribute to his life and work, edited by Ruth and Eddie Frow, and sponsored by the Amalgamated Union of Engineering Workers (Construction Section).

May I say as one volunteer, though only seventeen years of age at the time, I felt more confident through the example of other comrades who had left their families behind, their will to help others no matter what the cost to themselves, the deep comradeship and a profound belief in freedom and democracy.

So spoke Bernard McCormick, when in April 1990 at St Helens Town Hall, he unveiled a plaque commemorating the part played by him and five volunteers from St Helens who joined the British Battalion.

The marble plaque on the wall of the entrance foyer of the Town Hall, bears a simple inscription in gold impressed lettering with the legend adopted by the International Brigades: 'They shall not pass!', to commemorate those from the borough who 'fought to defend democracy' and lists six names.

The decision to erect a memorial to the volunteers was made by the St Helens Metropolitan Borough Council to honour the bravery and services of the volunteers to the cause of humanity. The Borough Council invited veterans, their relatives and friends to be present at the unveiling ceremony, first entertaining them to morning coffee and hosting a buffet lunch for its guests after the ceremony.

Council leader Marie Rimmer said it was a very great honour for the Borough Council to be involved in remembering those 'who fought in the International Brigade against fascism and Franco'. A veteran Brigader, Maurice Levine of Manchester, recalled being at a meeting in St Helens in 1938 to raise money to send an ambulance to Spain.

Bernard McCormick, the only surviving local veteran, joined the International Brigade in Liverpool where he was born. He was one of those who crossed from France into Spain over the Pyrenees under cover of darkness. After fighting in Spain for eleven months, he was repatriated because he was too young. A former Labour councillor of the Merseyside County Council, he moved to St Helens in the mid-sixties.

One whose name appears on the plaque was Bill Feeley, a singer, steel erector and active trade unionist, who died in 1977, in the middle of organizing a reunion of volunteer veterans. A staunch socialist all his life, he started the St Helens branch of the Amalgamated Union of Engineering Workers (Construction Section).

With two other St Helens men he set off for Spain in August 1937, made the Pyrenees night crossing, and after training was attached to a machine-gun company. He was wounded in the British Battalion's last battle on the Ebro front.

He was held in high esteem in the St Helens labour and trade union movement, and nearly 200 people attended his funeral. In November 1987 the St Helens Borough Council named a hall after him at the town's Trade Union Unemployed Resource Centre in College Street. It was inaugurated at a day-long celebration with over 100 present when speeches were made by local trade unionists and Bill Alexander, representing the International Brigade Association, followed by a play and folk-singing. Unfortunately, the centre no longer functions, but there still exist copies of a commemorative pamphlet to Bill Feeley, featuring his portrait in black and white on the cover, which was published in conjunction with the opening of the Bill Feeley Memorial Hall.

In it appears Bill Feeley's composition 'Honorary Membership Talking Blues', the last four lines of the last stanza of which speak for themselves:

> Joking apart, where workers combine,
> In demonstration or picket line
> To better their lot, those men from space
> You'll find, fightin' in Industry's Highest Place.

The memorial plaque on the wall of the foyer of St Helens Town Hall unveiled in April 1990, with Council leader Cllr Dave Watts shaking the hand of International Brigade veteran Bernard McCormick.

Ralph Fox Seat, Halifax

Halifax

It is sad for a man to die when he is so loved by the people.

These words are inscribed on a memorial plaque on a seat in Bull Green, Halifax, to honour Ralph Fox, who at the peak of his creative life was killed fighting for the Spanish Republican cause.

They were words spoken by him in 1936 at a memorial meeting for Maxim Gorky – and they form a fitting epitaph to Halifax's illustrious son.

Scarcely six weeks in Spain and just thirty-six, Ralph Fox fell on the Córdoba front in Southern Spain, stopping a Franco offensive on 3 January 1937. A political commissar, whose responsibility was to instil the highest fighting qualities in a unit and to see to the material and political needs of its members, he had been selected for the important task of training other political commissars, but asked to be released to go to the front. To honour his courage and leadership the Marseillaise Battalion was renamed the Ralph Fox Battalion. His commanding officer said Ralph Fox was 'an exceedingly brave man, and it was very largely due to his example that we

Ralph Fox, man of action and writer, a photograph taken in Southern Russia, probably in 1923, which appeared in his book People of the Steppes, *a personal narrative.*

were able to hold the enemy and save as many of our men as we did . . . he was a real hero.' German writer Alfred Kantorowicz, learning of his death, wrote in his diary that he 'seemed to me more and more of a model for us all, in his unobtrusive energy, modesty and determination in all matters of principle, in his straightforwardness and complete lack of vanity.'

Ralph Fox was born into a Halifax business family on 30 March 1900. He started writing poetry when still at school and graduated from Oxford with a first in modern languages. He was active in the Hands Off Russia movement and a founder member of the Communist Party. He joined the Friends Relief Mission in Southern Russia in 1923 and worked among the peasants of Samara. In 1925 he went back to work in the Far Eastern section of the Communist International, and again in 1929 when he worked as an English librarian in the Marx Engels Institute in Moscow. Three years later he was writing a regular column – Worker's Notebook – for the *Daily Worker*. He helped to found *Left Review* and *New Writing*. Among

The seat with the memorial plaque to Ralph Fox.

his literary output was a biography of Lenin, *Marxism and Modern Thought*, the study *Genghis Khan* and his influential *The Novel and the People*, which was published posthumously.

He was held in high esteem by his contemporaries. The poet Stephen Spender described his life and death 'as an example to us all', and the Poet Laureate C. Day Lewis noted that the 'conscience and integrity which inform all his writing compelled him to fight fascism and to die for human freedom'.

The Ralph Fox Memorial Committee was founded in Halifax in the years after the war. President of the Committee was the labour historian E.P. Thompson and vice-presidents were Dryden Brooke MP and Trades Council president Bob Spetch. Writer Florence Edwards was the secretary. At the inaugural meeting the Halifax Trades Council, the AEU district committee, the TGWU, National Council of Labour Colleges, Labour Party, Communist Party and the Old Boys Association from Fox's school, Heath Grammar School, were all represented.

The memorial plaque was first unveiled at a ceremony on 24 April 1950 when speeches were made by Dryden Brooke, Dr J.G. Crowther and Sam Lesser, a veteran of the British Battalion, and the hymn 'Jerusalem' was sung. The plaque was re-dedicated in 1979 when Sam Wild, the last commander of the British Battalion, unveiled it.

There followed annual Ralph Fox Memorial Lectures given by such prominent figures as the noted socialist G.D.H. Cole, Geoffrey Bing MP, Solly Sachs (general secretary of the South African Garment Workers' Union), Dona Torr (biographer of Tom Mann), Jim Figgins (NUR general secretary), prominent lawyer and MP D.N. Pritt QC, C. Day Lewis and Bert Ramelson (former national industrial organizer of the Communist Party).

The question arises, was it folly that young talents like Felicia Browne, Christopher Caudwell, John Cornford, Ralph Fox and David Guest should have been cut short when perhaps their very original gifts could have been used to far greater effect in the same cause?

The people of Halifax did not think so, nor did these young people. Convinced anti-fascists, they felt their place was alongside other anti-fascists defending the Spanish Republic – their example inspired others of their generation to fight heroically for the cause of liberty.

In his *Novel and the People*, Ralph Fox explained: 'It is our fortune to have been born at one of those moments in history which demand from each one of us as an individual that he make his private decision . . . he cannot stand aside, and by our actions we shall extend our imagination, because we shall have been true to the passions in us.'

The memorial plaque on the seat in Bull Green, Halifax, to Ralph Fox.

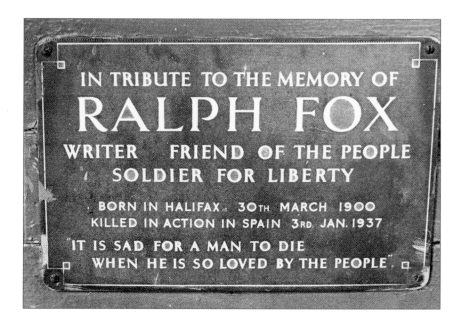

IN TRIBUTE TO THE MEMORY OF
RALPH FOX
WRITER   FRIEND OF THE PEOPLE
SOLDIER FOR LIBERTY

BORN IN HALIFAX. 30TH. MARCH 1900
KILLED IN ACTION IN SPAIN 3RD. JAN. 1937

"IT IS SAD FOR A MAN TO DIE
WHEN HE IS SO LOVED BY THE PEOPLE".

Rotherham Peace Garden

Behind us was the ground where the best of our comrades had fallen. Pitiful little mounds of earth along the roadside indicated the last resting place of dozens of our valiant comrades. . . . now we were back on the same ground again; forced to surrender the territory that we had paid so dearly for. But it was not lack of courage, men or leadership that forced us to relinquish that ground and lose so many comrades; the men responsible were those friends of Franco who sit upon the Non-Intervention Committee. If we had had sufficient aeroplanes and heavy guns we would not have given up one inch of ground let alone surrendered Brunete.

Rotherham

Moving and angry words from *Pounded Earth*, an account of his fighting in Spain written by Rotherham International Brigader Tommy James, which appears together with the biography *Tommy James — A Lion of a Man* by Brian Lewis and Bill Gledhill.

Tommy James, a First World War veteran, often arrested for his political activities and a foundation member of the Communist Party, spent his life helping workers to know and fight for their rights. He was an anti-fascist who put his beliefs into practice in Spain. He was made a Freeman of Rotherham, posthumously.

In 1950 in Sheffield it was appropriately Tommy James who welcomed the great Spanish painter Pablo Picasso, who had produced the masterpiece *Guernica* — an angry and powerful protest at the callous fascist bombing of the Spanish town. Picasso had come to participate in the World Peace Congress — breaking the ban imposed by Attlee's Labour Government on foreign delegates to the congress, which had to be transferred to Warsaw.

The Rotherham Peace Garden showing the memorial seat and stone obelisk dedicated to Tommy James.

In April 1985 Rotherham citizens placed a memorial plaque on a bench seat to Tommy James on a plot of ground they called the Peace Garden, at the corner of Wharncliffe Street and Doncaster Road. The plaque reads:

Tommy James: Born 1898 Rotherham Workhouse
Fighter for Peace and Freedom
1913–1918 Soldier in First World War
1920–1936 Unemployed and Hunger Marches
          Local Leader in General Strike
1936–1937 Fighter in Spanish Civil War
1937–1939 Public Agitator College Square
1967–1971 President of Rotherham Trades Union Council
Worker Writer Socialist
Died 1971

In February 1986 on the 50th anniversary of the election of the Popular Front Government in Spain a memorial stone obelisk was erected on the plot. The base of the obelisk is inscribed with the word Peace, in English, Russian, German and Japanese respectively on its four faces, and on a plaque below is the legend: 'We tread but one path. This open space is dedicated to the memory of Tommy James, Man of Rotherham, 1898–1971.'

In a further tribute to him in 1986, Sheffield Popular Theatre put on *Deepest Red*, a dramatization of Tommy James's account of his time in Spain with the International Brigade. A prize at Rotherham Community College and the Trade Union Library at Sheffield's Wortley Hall carry his name.

TOMMY JAMES BORN 1898 ROTHERHAM WORKHOUSE
FIGHTER FOR PEACE AND FREEDOM.

1915–1918 SOLDIER IN 1st WORLD WAR   1937–1939 PUBLIC AGITATOR COLLEGE SQUARE

1920–1936 UNEMPLOYED AND HUNGER MARCHES   1967–1971 PRESIDENT OF ROTHERHAM
LOCAL LEADER IN GENERAL STRIKE   TRADES UNION COUNCIL

1936–1937 FIGHTER IN SPANISH CIVIL WAR

WORKER WRITER SOCIALIST   DIED 1971

Close-ups of the memorial plaque which describes Tommy James as 'Worker Writer Socialist' and the bench seat to which it is attached.

Close-up of the stone obelisk.

Leeds City Hall

J. Dutton returned from Spain to Leeds to continue the fight against fascisim.

For Leeds one Remembrance Day is of very special significance – that held on 11 November 1989. For on that Saturday morning Leeds City Council honoured its twenty heroes who volunteered to go to Spain.

A memorial to the eight men who gave their lives on Spanish soil and the twelve who came back to continue the struggle against fascism was erected in the form of a plaque, bearing their names, in the foyer of the City Hall.

Present at the unveiling ceremony were Barbara Durkhop (Spanish Member of the European Parliament), representatives of Leeds' twin town – Dortmund, Councillor Jon Trickett (leader of the council), Leeds Brigade veteran Alan Harris, Brigade veterans from different areas, and local councillors and representatives of the labour and trade union movement.

Spain had a profound effect on a very broad stratum of British people, arousing deep emotions, admiration and solidarity. Leeds was one of the main centres of the hugely successful and very broad Aid Spain movement in the 1930s. Jim Fyrth in his book *The Signal Was Spain*, about the Aid Spain movement 1936–9, relates how Sam Wagenheim, a shop steward at Montagu Burton's factory in Leeds, placed a tin of milk on the centre of the cutters' table where he worked as a tailor with a piece of cardboard stating 'Milk for Spain'. The idea caught on with machinists following his example and some workers put cardboard boxes for milk and coins at the factory exits. Within a week there was enough milk to fill a pantechnicon which was driven out to Spain. As demonstrations and rallies in support of the young Spanish Republic spread throughout the country, there was a 600-strong meeting held in Leeds Town Hall square.

There was also a strong anti-fascist movement in the city and even after the Second World War there were regular open-air meetings on the City Hall steps denouncing thirty-five years of Franco terror against the Spanish people. A regular speaker at these meetings was Bert Ramelson, who had fought in Spain with the International Brigade and was for many years the Yorkshire district secretary of the Communist Party and its national industrial organizer.

It was Alan Harris who, with Sam Wagenheim, campaigned for Leeds to erect a memorial to fellow Brigaders. A keen rambler and cyclist, an active member of the Labour League of Youth, he fought against Mosley's Blackshirts on the streets of Leeds. He was twenty-five when he joined the 15th Brigade in

Spain, explaining that the atmosphere 'at that time was dangerous and exciting. We felt anything could happen.'

He was thrown in at the deep end. Having only fired a rifle six times in training, he found himself at the front line with fellow volunteers. He later described how 'the bullets started whizzing over. Someone shouted: "They're coming!" Tanks and lorries were racing down the road. We started firing like mad. Someone set a tank on fire and a cheer went right along the line. Then suddenly they were behind us.'

Alan Harris came home safely, but his friend Walt Dobson, with whom he set out for Spain, was one of the eight who did not return. Another was Phil Elias who was shot in cold blood by a fascist officer when he was taken prisoner.

Returning to Leeds in 1939, Alan Harris recalled a huge crowd waiting at Leeds station. 'I was treated as a hero and carried shoulder high to a reception at the Co-op rooms.'

The memorial in the foyer of Leeds City Hall unveiled by Bill Alexander on 11 November 1989.

Sheffield City Hall

Sheffield

The memorial plaque set in a large block of roughly hewn Pennine rock in the Peace Garden by Sheffield City Hall.

Sheffield, the 'city of steel', not only one of the great industrial centres of Britain, but also one of the great arsenals of the world, has another aspect – an outstanding record in the cause of peace going back to before the First World War, and a record second to none in the fight against fascism.

In June 1934 a demonstration of 15,000 voiced opposition to a meeting in the City Hall of Sir Oswald Mosley and his British Union of Fascists. The demonstration was organized by the Communist Party, the Independent Labour Party and the National Unemployed Workers' Movement. In August the city was the venue for a National Youth

Congress against Fascism and War, which filled the City Hall with delegates from all over Britain.

Hundreds of leaflets dropped from a plane over the city declared: 'You have been bombed . . . by leaflets . . . Today they are leaflets! Tomorrow they could be bombs . . .'

Over 1,800 people in Sheffield distributed voting papers for the National Peace Ballot in 1935 and 149,347 people voted, the overwhelming majority for arms reduction and banning of arms manufacture for profit. Sheffield set up a peace council.

SPANIARDS' VALOUR EXPLAINED BY CITY VOLUNTEER

A Sheffield man who has spent some months fighting in the International Brigade in Spain, Mr. Josef Albaya, of 833, Chesterfield road, Woodseats, told a "Daily Independent" reporter last night that he believed the Spanish Government had every reason for claiming that they would be able to turn out a 'plane a day by October.

As an interpreter, he travelled much in Spain, but met very few Russians.

"I must admit I went there expecting to find many Russians, but I found very few Russian - speaking people, and most of those were Poles."

He said the few Russians who were among the Government forces were technicians and drivers.

While the International Column held the Nationalists back at the beginning of the war, the Government forces had been trained. They were now able to fight for themselves.

Mr. Josef Albaya.

ADMIRED SPANISH GRIT

Josef Albaya.

In 1936 Sheffield formed its own Left Book Club and an Aid to Spain committee was formed with a nucleus of club members. In the winter of 1936/7 public meetings were held to raise money, medical aid and food for Spain. The entire labour and trade union movement rallied in support of the Republican cause in Spain and had the backing of the Church through the Bishop of Sheffield and other religious dignitaries.

In June and July 1986 an ambitious programme of events was held at various venues devoted to the anti-fascist war in Spain, including exhibitions of photographs and posters, an exhibition presenting the story of Picasso's masterpiece *Guernica*, plays, poetry recitals, lectures and a documentary on the war and its causes, narrated by Sir John Gielgud.

The central event was the unveiling of a beautiful memorial plaque set in a large block of roughly hewn Pennine rock in the Peace Garden outside the City Hall on which the inscription reads:

In honour of the Sheffield men who fought alongside the Spanish people in their struggle for democracy and of the men and women in the city who worked in support of the cause.

> Yet, Freedom yet, thy banner torn but flying
> Streams like the thunder-storm against the wind.   Byron

Seven men from Sheffield fought in the International Brigade in Spain, and two were killed in the fighting. One of those was Arthur Newsome, one of two children of Arthur, a drayman, and his wife Eliza, who lived in a long cobbled street. He left school in 1926 at the age of fourteen against the background of the General Strike. Youth being a source of cheap labour, he soon found himself in a rolling mill. He joined the Young Communist League and was caught up in events like the 1932 unemployed demonstrations. He was a participant in the historic Kinder trespass that year. In the period 1935–6 he was involved in anti-fascist activities, campaigning for peace and took part in the 1936 Hunger March.

Involved in collecting food for Spain, he volunteered to fight with the International Brigade. In Spain he was soon under fire and found himself in early January 1937 on the Jaen front near Córdoba in Andalucia. He and several of his comrades were strafed from the air by the fascists as they lay in their trenches. An Irish volunteer dragged Newsome's badly wounded body for 200 yards to a field station, but he was dead on arrival.

Shortly after, several hundred mourners wearing red badges with black centres packed the city Memorial Hall in Sheffield. A black and white banner depicting Arthur Newsome's head stated: 'We have lost a comrade – he died fighting for freedom and democracy.'

One of those to return to Sheffield from Spain was Josef Albaya. Born in 1911 to a family that had emigrated to Britain from the Basque area of

Spain, he had a double motive for volunteering to fight in Spain – a deep belief in democracy and a strong attachment to his family origins. As a young man he followed political events in Spain closely. During the autumn of 1936, Joe Albaya listened nightly to broadcasts from Radio Madrid and as the family spoke Spanish at home, he was able to appreciate the stirring call of La Pasionaria to workers, peasants and anti-fascists to support the Republic. He told his family he had decided to join the International Brigade and his wife Win Albaya later recalled: 'The week before Christmas 1936, Joe came to my home to say goodbye. Most partings are sad, but this was unusually so, due to the combined elements of uncertainty and unknown dangers. The virtual blackout of his movements from then, until a link of communication was restored, made that period one of the blackest I can remember.'

He took part in the historic Jarama Battle and said of his experience: 'I advanced when I was told to advance and retreated when I was told to retreat.' Speaking French and Spanish fairly fluently, he acted as interpreter and was fully occupied, regularly travelling miles to get supplies for the International Brigades, and sometimes working 24 hours a day. On his return to Sheffield he soon adjusted to civilian life, and spoke freely about his experience in Spain, although his wife pointed out: 'I soon found that there were certain "no-go" areas, chiefly concerning the Jarama Battle and other matters, which I learned to respect and on which I never ventured to press him, and this reticence continued all his life.'

He entered teaching and became a member of the National Union of Teachers. He died several years ago.

Hull City Hall

Hull

My sons, be decisive always: if they ask you if you are Red, say plainly you are proletarian, poor, human and Christian . . . that wicked men infringe the sacred mandates and declare war on us, and that if this is being Red, as the murderers say, then we are Red. We are Red as the poppy, but we are Red because they have shed our blood, and our bodies are stained with the red that runs in our veins.

This is part of a letter from a Basque father to his sons in 1937, recorded in *The Signal was Spain* by Jim Fyrth, in the chapter on the 4,200 Basque refugee children who arrived in Southampton on the Spanish ship *Habana* in May 1937.

Two months later, twenty-two of the boys and eighteen of the girls were warmly welcomed when they arrived at Paragon Station in Hull by the lord mayor and lady mayoress, the youth committee of the Regal Cinema Mickey Mouse Club and other groups. The *Hull Daily Mail* reported that 'Hull could not have given them a greater welcome if they had been 40 Cabinet Ministers'. The Joint Committee for Spanish Aid set up in Hull by Frida Stewart with help from Hull University academics established a Basque Children's Committee which ran the home for the refugees. At weekends the children, some as young as five, stayed with Hull families. Some were taken in by local builder Robert Tarran. As the anti-fascist war continued more refugees arrived and were cared for.

There was enormous sympathy and support for the Spanish Republican cause in Hull. Soon after the anti-fascist war started, a Hull City Labour Party Spain Committee, established with representatives from all the four constituency parties on Humberside and support from the trades council, sponsored a number of fund-raising events. Other organizations such as the Left Book Club, the Socialist Youth Club (a meeting ground for the Labour League of Youth and Young Communist League) were also involved in collecting food street by street. The Joint Committee organized a Humberside Foodship for Spain. Large gifts of dried fish were received for the ship from Hull fishermen. A benefit football match was held and a Lord Mayor's Appeal started. An important part in the success of the Humberside foodship was played by the Archbishop of York and the Bishop of Ripon.

In April 1990 a plaque bearing the names of the eight Hull International Brigaders, four of whom were killed in Spain, was unveiled at the Guild Hall at a ceremony attended by the Lord Mayor John Stanley, the only surviving local veteran Richard Mortimer, relatives and friends of the volunteers and representatives of the International Brigade Association.

Richard Mortimer, who was then living in Portsmouth, expressed pleasure about the plaque, saying: 'I am glad it has come from my home town.'

One of those in attendance was Maria de los Angeles, then aged sixty-six and married. One of the Basque children given shelter in Hull, she decided to stay on there. Another person at the ceremony was former lord mayor and city councillor, Violet Mitchell, one of the people who took the Basque children

into their homes and knew some of the men who went to Spain from Hull. She was among those who campaigned for the memorial plaque to be erected.

Hull men Rob Wardle and James Bentley were killed when the British Battalion ran into a powerful Italian column of Mussolini's tanks and armoured cars at Calaceite. Rob Wardle junior was determined to see where his father died fighting fascism and travelled with his wife Audrey to Calaceite in 1992. They took with them a small plaque with the inscription in English and Spanish: 'In memory of Robert Wardle aged 28 and James Bentley aged 24 from Hull, England, volunteer soldiers in the British Battalion of the 15th International Brigade. Killed in action Calaceite March 31st 1938 Salud.' In Calaceite the Wardles were received at the town hall and met Mercedes, daughter of one of the twelve victims murdered by the fascists in Calaceite who, seventeen at the time, had her head shaved by the fascists. The plaque has been set in the wall over the burial place of Mercedes' murdered father.

Morris Miller, another Hull man, who became assistant battalion political commissar to Bob Cooney, was killed in the last offensive across the Ebro in August 1938 in the Pandols sector, when the fascists launched an attack of unprecedented severity, with the artillery sounding like a continuous roll of thunder. Bill Alexander in *Volunteers for Liberty* described how when the barrage stopped 'the enemy infantry – nearly two battalion

A group of Basque children enjoying the sunshine at their camp at Shoreham just after their arrival from Spain.

Rob Wardle pointing to the name of his father on the memorial plaque in Hull Guild Hall.

strong – attacked. However the British, although much reduced in numbers and half shell-shocked and deafened by the bombardment, repulsed the assault and did not give an inch.'

One of those to return after fighting in Spain, Joe Latus, a Hull fisherman, commanded a boat running supplies to the liberation forces in Greece during the Second World War.

This plaque honours the memory

of the volunteers

from

Kingston upon Hull

who fought with the International Brigade

in Spain during the war against fascism

1936 – 1939

J. ATKINSON killed JARAMA February 1937

JIM BENTLEY killed GANDESA April 1938

MORRIS MILLER killed EBRO August 1938

ROBERT WARDLE killed GANDESA April 1938

JOE LATUS returned

RICHARD MORTIMER returned

SAM WALTERS returned

LESLIE WILSON returned

Stoke-on-Trent Town Hall

Stoke-on-Trent

Man hardened clay into a bowl before he spun flax and made a garment, and the last lone man will want an earthen vessel after he has abandoned his ruined house for a cave, and his woven rags for an animal's skin. This supremacy of the most ancient of crafts is in the secret nature of things, and cannot be explained.

So wrote Arnold Bennett about the antiquity of the potter's craft in *Anna of the Five Towns*. That ancient skill was called upon when Stoke-on-Trent City Council decided to allocate £600 for a commemorative plaque fashioned in ceramic to honour the local volunteers who fought in the ranks of the International Brigade.

The simple but beautiful plaque on the wall in the foyer of Stoke Town Hall was unveiled at a ceremony on 7 September 1989. Inscribed on it are the names of five men, three of whom, H.T. Bosley, J.P. Burley and L. O'Nichen were killed in battles on the Ebro and at Tortosa. In a folder announcing the unveiling, the leader of the city council, Ronald Southern, said it was a 'privilege' to honour the five men who had fought side by side with the Spanish people.

The memorial was suggested by a former Hanley lecturer Mike Rennie and International Brigader, Dave Goodman, originally from Middlesbrough, who eventually made his home in the Potteries. Dave Goodman also persuaded Stoke City Council to hold a series of annual memorial lectures. The first was given in February 1994 by Rodney Bickerstaffe, UNISON trade union leader, on the theme 'Learning the Lesson: No Fascist Revival'. It was attended by the deputy lord mayor and the deputy chair of Staffordshire Council, councillors and local trade union leaders.

In 1995 over 300 people packed the City Museum lecture theatre, along with the lord mayor and other civic leaders from the city and neighbouring boroughs of Newcastle-under-Lyme, Leek, Stafford and Staffs County Council, when the second memorial lecture was given by veteran socialist Tony Benn MP. Also present at the lecture were five members, covering three generations, of the family of Reg Grocott, one of the five local volunteers who fought in Spain.

Dave Goodman, an active communist and anti-fascist aged twenty-two, who was smuggled across the Pyrenees into Spain in 1938, was taken prisoner by Franco's forces during the crucial two-month bitterly fought battle when Teruel was lost to the fascists. Confined in a concentration camp for nearly a year, he described the camp as being 'very high up and bitterly cold even in summer, it was louse-ridden, flea-ridden and rat-ridden.'

Opposite: The ceramic memorial plaque in the foyer of the Town Hall in Stoke-on-Trent, unveiled on 7 September 1989.

This plaque commemorates the volunteers

from

THE CITY OF STOKE · ON · TRENT

who fought with the International Brigade

in Spain during the war against Fascism

1936 - 1939

H.T.BOSLEY	Killed Ebro	July 1938
J.P.BURLEY	Killed Tortosa	March 1938
L.ONICHAN	Killed Ebro	June 1938

J.CALLEN   R.GROCOTT

Nottinghamshire County Hall

Nottinghamshire County Hall is surrounded by trees and lawns, it is pleasant and peaceful. People who have business there, as they walk by its walls are reminded of men who went from their county to try to ensure that today's generation could live in peace.

On the walls are bronze plaques. One is a sculpted relief of bombed and shattered buildings, another carries the legend:

> In honour of the volunteers who left Nottinghamshire to fight in the International Brigade, Spain 1936–1939. They fought alongside the Spanish people to stop fascism and save liberty and peace for all. They went because their eyes could see no other way. No Pasaran.

Two more plaques list the names of five volunteers who were killed and where they died and the names of the thirteen who returned to continue the struggle.

It says something for the understanding and good sense of the people of the county that despite a heated controversy breaking out when it was proposed that the County Council should erect a memorial to the International Brigaders – some contrary views being expressions of genuine reservation, but others quite malicious politically – the memorial was duly commissioned from a young Doncaster sculptor Michael Johnson, installed and then unveiled at a ceremony on 24 September 1993.

The ceremony was attended by His Excellency Alberto Aza, the Spanish Ambassador to Britain, Councillor Dennis Pettitt, leader of the council, county and city dignitaries, national IBA leaders and countless friends and relatives of the volunteers.

The speech and very presence of the Spanish Ambassador bore out the truth of the words of Spanish Prime Minister Juan Negrin to the League of Nations in 1938 when the International Brigades were withdrawn and he spoke of 'courageous and devoted men who, in an outburst of generosity that will never be forgotten by the Spanish people, came to its help at one of the most critical hours in its national history'.

Among those present were two Brigaders. Walter Gregory, who left for Spain at twenty-four, his only military training being a summer with the British Army. 'I was heavily involved in left-wing politics in Nottingham. The Spanish republicans who were defending democracy, said they needed doctors, nurses and soldiers, so I went,' said Walter Gregory. Wounded in three battles, taken to hospital, captured by the

Walter Gregory, who was wounded in three battles.

fascists, imprisoned and sentenced to death, he was eventually repatriated in 1939 in exchange for some Italian prisoners.

Lionel Jacobs, a well-known figure in Nottingham and former president of the Nottingham Trades Council said he had been 'fighting the fascists in the streets of London' so going to Spain was for him the continuation of the same fight. He also went without any military training.

In a battle near Gandesa, Lionel Jacobs and some hundred of his fellow volunteers were trapped between Italian tanks and infantry, and taken prisoner. He too was later exchanged for Italian prisoners and repatriated in 1939. 'I would do the same again. You have to do what your conscience dictates,' he said.

Left to right: Leader of the County Council, Cllr Dennis Pettitt, the Spanish Ambassador Alberto Aza and Jack Jones standing in front of the sculpted relief of bombed-out buildings, part of the memorial set in the exterior wall of Nottinghamshire County Hall.

St Thomas Peace Garden, Birmingham

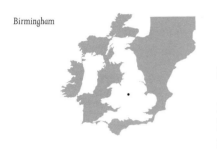

Birmingham

In 1936 the Birmingham Labour weekly, *The Town Crier*, reporting a united Bull Ring demonstration, carried the headline: 'SPAIN IS OUR PROBLEM – Our Turn Next if Democracy is Defeated' and a further headline: 'BIRMINGHAM RALLYING TO SUPPORT SPANISH WORKERS.'

Birmingham knew something about the danger of fascism. Oswald Mosley was a Birmingham Labour MP in the twenties. After he formed his British Union of Fascists he returned to the city in 1934 and addressed a rally at Bingley Hall to a fanfare, with 2,000 of his followers shouting 'Heil!' At the May Day Rally that followed, marchers chanted anti-BUF slogans and when Mosley returned for a rally in 1935 he was met by determined anti-fascist resistance.

Birmingham rallied to support the Spanish people's fight against fascism because it had militant and democratic working-class traditions: support for the famous 'dockers' tanner' strike in London in 1889, the fight for trade unionism at the turn of the century, strikes for a living wage, solid stand in the 1926 General Strike, and the struggle against the means test and organizing the unemployed.

Birmingham knows something about the need for peace too. The Second World War, the 'war for democracy', brought bombs to Birmingham, one of the worst affected areas of the city being Sparkbrook, where one house in eighteen was totally destroyed.

St Thomas Peace Garden, Birmingham, with the IBA memorial in the centre colonnade.

Hence on 2 December 1992, despite rain pouring down, the multi-racial peoples of Birmingham in their national costumes, led by the lord mayor and Bishop of Birmingham in their colourful robes, paid tribute to the eighteen International Brigaders who went from the city to Spain. A memorial plaque was unveiled to them by veteran Brigader Jack Jones, former TGWU general secretary and pensioners' leader.

It was a striking endorsement of the slogan at the time when the volunteers set out for Spain, 'Save Spain, Save Peace', for the plaque is on the colonnade, a major feature of the beautiful St Thomas Peace Garden built on the war ruins of the old church. The Peace Garden was formally opened by the lord mayor that day. Its nineteen plaques have peace messages from major world faiths, from various countries and from cities abroad. Three primary school choirs sang 'Make me a channel of your peace.'

> Build the road of peace before us
> Build it wide and deep and long.

These are words of 'Ode to Joy' by Paul Robeson, that great fighter for peace, which was sung on 2 December by those who came to honour the volunteers. The singing was led by the Clarion Singers, one of the founders of which was International Brigader Dr Colin Bradsworth on his

The memorial plaque.

return from medical duties at the front in Spain. The choir popularized Spanish Republican songs in the campaign to aid Spain.

A lone survivor from the Birmingham volunteers, Ted Smallbone, was present that day. He was dismissed by Cadburys in 1937 because of his political activities, was wounded on the Ebro front and returned in 1938.

Among those who volunteered from Birmingham was Bert Williams, a Welsh ex-miner, member of the Central Committee and Midlands organizer of the Communist Party. In Spain he was one of the British Battalion political commissars who played an outstanding role in very difficult circumstances.

Leicester Peace Walk

Leicester

In Leicester's Victoria Park, off University Road, is an area designated as a Peace Walk. At a ceremony on 15 February 1993 watched by some 200 people a memorial was unveiled to honour three local men who fought with the International Brigade in Spain and were killed out there. It is a simple, but beautiful, polished grey granite tablet set on a base on the lawn on one side of the Peace Walk. The granite has cut into it traditional laurel leaves on either side to decorate the inscription in gold letters, which reads:

> To the honour and memory of the Leicester members of the International Brigades who died fighting fascism in Spain, 1936–1939
>> Fred Sykes Jarama 1937
>> Jack Watson Jarama 1937
>> Roy Watts Ebro 1938
>> Spain
>> No Pasaran!

The appeal for the memorial was launched in 1990 by the Leicester Socialist Centre, a non-sectarian resources centre whose members are left-wing and trade unionists. The memorial cost £750 and donations for it came from the Socialist Centre, the Leicester Secular Society (the oldest secular society in the world – founded in 1851), and from public sector unions NALGO and NUPE, shop workers' union USDAW, transport union TGWU and the Alternative Services Co-operative. In addition there were many gifts from individuals, underlining the wide sympathy and support the project attracted.

Roy Watts, who worked for the Leicester Co-operative Society, was a member of both the Leicester Secular Society and the Labour League of Youth.

He was wounded in the advance when Republican forces stormed across the fast-flowing Ebro, deep into Franco-held territory in an attempt to end the division of Spain into two parts. The British Battalion, a part of the 15th Brigade, was involved in this engagement.

Franco rallied an immense force of German and Italian aircraft, dominating the air by day and night. The wounded could only be evacuated at night, making the hazardous journey across the pontoon bridge which was being bombed constantly. The wounded were then treated in an emergency hospital in a railway tunnel. Many of the wounded had fractured bones and serious flesh wounds.

Roy Watts wrote, after being wounded, from his hospital bed to a fellow worker at the Co-operative Society describing the treatment he was receiving. He was referring to a method of treatment developed by an Austrian surgeon, Bohler, in Vienna, which the British doctor Alex Tudor Hart introduced when treating the wounded in Spain. Essentially it involved encasing the affected limb in plaster after all the infected flesh had been cut away and the wound sutured. It was then left to heal.

TO THE HONOUR AND MEMORY
OF THE LEICESTER MEMBERS
OF THE INTERNATIONAL BRIGADES
WHO DIED FIGHTING FASCISM IN SPAIN
1936 – 1939

FRED SYKES
JARAMA 1937

JACK WATSON
JARAMA 1937

ROY WATTS
EBRO 1938
SPAIN

¡ NO PASARAN !

*Two little girls stay to gaze and wonder by the
memorial and its floral tributes in Peace Walk, in
Leicester's Victoria Park, off University Road.*

City Centre, Reading

The cover of the programme for the memorial unveiling ceremony.

How many mothers in Spain, in England and countless other lands grieved for the sons they had borne who fell on Spanish soil fighting for the cause of liberty and peace? They were legion.

Mother Spain in 1939 grieved for her dead son – the young Republic. Today her proud, upright image clasping in her arms her dead son, stands in front of the Civic Centre, in Castle Street, Reading. On the reverse side are carved in relief three heads – heads of sons of Reading mothers. Sons who died fighting to save the life of the young Spanish Republic.

Standing five feet high, the memorial bears the names of the seven Reading volunteers who fought or served in the medical teams with the International Brigade in Spain and returned, and the names of three who fought and did not return – William Ball, Archibald (Josh) Francis and George Middleton – and incorporates the date and place of their deaths.

The sculpture was made by Eric Stanford, a former student of St Martin's School of Art, London, and of the Fine Art department of Reading University. By a strange but appropriate coincidence, he received his first lesson in carving from José Alberdt who, as a young boy, was a refugee from Spain in this country. Eric Stanford, Keeper of Art at Reading Museum, was given a year off by Reading Borough Council to make the memorial, which was funded by the Reading International Brigade Memorial Committee. When asked to make the memorial, Eric Stanford, a former Labour councillor, expressed delight, saying it was 'the most exciting thing I have ever been asked to do'.

The memorial, the culmination of a seven year campaign, including a packed Reading Town Hall meeting in 1986, was unveiled at a ceremony on 5 May 1990 by the Mayor of Reading, Maureen Lockey. Hundreds participated in the ceremony, among whom were Brigade veterans, including volunteers from Reading, Dr Reginald Saxon, Jimmy Moon, who was taken prisoner by Franco's fascists, and Thora Silverthorne, who served as a nurse close to the front throughout the war in Spain. Local actor Tom Radcliffe recited from the poem 'Requiem Mass' by Jack Lindsay and the ceremony concluded with the singing of 'Jarama', led by opera singer Stella Higgins and local folk-singer Quentin Kean.

The memorial committee expressed its sincere appreciation for the generous help of the Reading Borough Council, the masons A.F. Jones, Lansing-Linde of Basingstoke, who transported the finished memorial to the site and Bulmershe Court of Reading University, who provided a studio for the sculptor to work in.

*Front and back of the Reading memorial sculpted
by Eric Stanford, unveiled on 5 May 1990 by
Reading Mayor Cllr Maureen Lockey.*

University of Kent, Canterbury

How did people get into Spain? Here is an instructive and highly amusing account:

> I went round to King Street to see a hush-hush man called Comrade Robson; he was the person in charge of volunteers for Spain because it was highly illegal at that time . . . Robson said to me: 'Well, look here; you're a student, you know Paris,' and I said, 'Well I don't know Paris.' He said, 'Anyway you know French' and I said, 'Well I know a little French' and he said, 'Well I want you to guide this party across to Paris and I will give very careful instructions.' I suppose I must have taken notes – I can't remember – but he gave very, very careful instructions about what I was to do when we got to Paris and how I was to throw people off the scent, by travelling on the Metro in the wrong direction and then changing stations and so on and after wending my way backwards and forwards through Paris, I was to arrive at Aubervilliers.

Tony McLean, chairman of the North Kensington Communist Party branch, did eventually make it to Spain to join the International Brigade. His description of the May Day demonstration in London before he left gives a vivid picture of the prevailing atmosphere about Spain:

> It was an extremely colourful demonstration; very large numbers of girls were selling Spanish literature and were dressed as 'militanios' and we had Spanish Republic colours all over the place. Spain was the theme of the demonstration and I think there were about 50,000 of us. . . . I was particularly struck, if I may say so, by the United Christian Left which had four enormous great figures in cardboard, larger than life . . . one was John Ball, I remember, another one was Winstanley of the Diggers, a third one was George Loveless of the Tolpuddle Martyrs and the fourth one was a Basque Nationalist, you know, a Basque patriot.

In Spain Tony McLean, who spoke French and Spanish, helped as an interpreter, gave political lectures, was attached as a research worker at the International Brigade training centre at Albacete and at the Battalion training base at Madrigueras, and worked in the International Brigade censor section at Barcelona. He described his work in the research bureau as establishing what had happened to people in the International Brigade, who had been killed or admitted to hospital. This was important for International Brigade records as well as for relatives wanting information.

Following his return from Spain he spoke and lectured on Spain at numerous meetings in Nottinghamshire, quite a number of them for the WEA, miners' welfare and other organizations.

He was a lifelong supporter and tutor in adult education; his interest was in humanities and art history and the Spanish anti-fascist war. He was appointed as full-time adult tutor for the University of Oxford in 1945, following his war service, and for many years was that university's Senior Tutor in Kent. When he helped to transfer responsibility for adult education to the new University of Kent at Canterbury, he himself transferred to the new university and remained in the post of Senior Tutor until he retired in 1975 at the age of sixty-seven. For the years until his death he continued to teach part-time extensively.

Over 200 attended his funeral service at Maidstone in October 1982 and in the following January a Tony McLean Memorial Fund was set up by his colleagues for bursaries to students to help them with their residential course fees. By September over £5,000 had been raised. Now the annual income from the Memorial Fund is about £500 and the number of beneficiaries annually averages twenty – most for one or two residential courses run by the University of Kent's School of Continuing Education or by the South Eastern District WEA.

In the grounds of the university there is a memorial seat and plaque to commemorate Tony McLean, with the inscription: 'And gladly wolde he lerne & gladly teche.' It is a tribute not only to his tremendous contribution to adult education in Kent, but also to his humanity and democratic convictions which led him to serve the cause of liberty in Spain.

Standing around the memorial seat to Tony McLean in the grounds of the University of Kent, Canterbury, are, left to right: Alec Barbrook (then director of the School of Continuing Education, UKC), Prof Maurice Vile, Christopher McLean (Tony McLean's brother), Margaret McLean (Tony McLean's widow), John Todd (then Master of Rutherford College, UKC) and John Woolford.

Castle Park, Bristol

Bristol

Winifred Sandford from Castle Cary in Somerset, at the ripe old age of eighty-eight, made a special pilgrimage to Bristol early in December 1986, to honour those who had died in Spain fighting in the International Brigade. The occasion was the unveiling of a plaque set in the wall in the city's Castle Park in the presence of Lord Mayor, Councillor Joan Jones, city councillors, International Brigade veterans and prominent local people.

The plaque's inscription reads:

Spanish Civil War 1936–39. This plaque was erected by Bristol City Council to commemorate those British volunteers who fought with the Republican Army in the Spanish Civil War. The 526 volunteers from Britain who gave their lives to defend democracy included four men from Bristol. They died for Liberty.

> W.G. Boyce January 1938
> J. Burton February 1937
> L. Huson May 1938
> T.E. Stephens July 1938

This plaque was unveiled on 11th December 1986 by Mr Jack Jones, CH, General Secretary of the TGWU 1969 to 1978 and member of the International Brigade.

Winifred Sandford was living in the Pyrenees mountains with her husband, novelist Ralph Bates, when Franco started his rebellion against the young Spanish Republic. She worked with nurses in the medical sections. She could speak Spanish fluently and was a journalist and broadcaster in Barcelona, but from July 1937 she began to work for the Spanish Medical Aid Committee for a time as a reporter, photographer, courier and 'Responsabile' – a sort of personnel officer – for the nurses. Her work involved a good deal of travelling in munition trucks and convoys until she was provided with a car. She helped produce a regular bulletin.

In *The Signal was Spain* she is quoted by the author Jim Fyrth as saying of the forty British and American nurses who came into her care: 'About half of them when they came out were quite unaware of the historical importance of the war and its international complications. They were just nurses, courageous women, willing to work under the most dangerous conditions. The other half knew what it was about . . .'

Interviewed by the *Bristol Evening Post* at the unveiling, she explained that 'you were expected to help with everything. I helped with medical operations and transporting the wounded. Sometimes I just sat down at the side of the road to give my blood. . . . The war provided me with so many vivid memories.'

Another person at the unveiling was someone who played an important role in organizing Aid for Spain in the 1930s. He was Bill Nicholas, who,

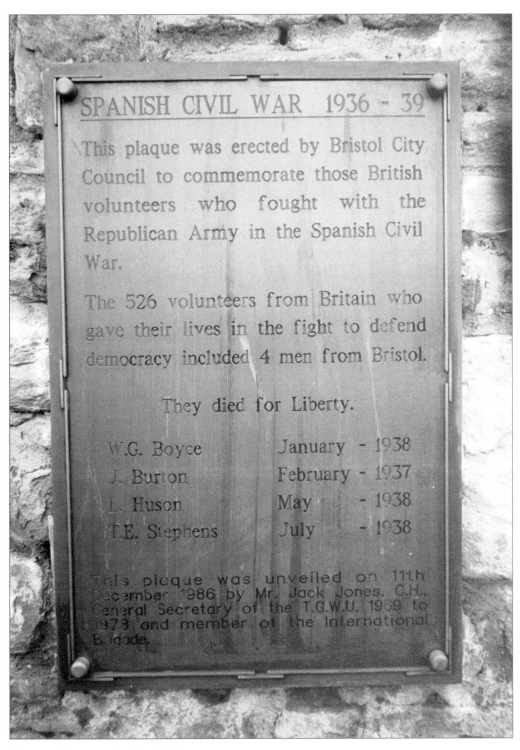

The memorial plaque set in the wall in Bristol's
Castle Park, unveiled in December 1986.

as the 22-year-old chairman of the Labour League of Youth in Bristol East, was one of a group of young Bristol socialists who met to discuss help for the Spanish people fighting Franco fascism. This was understandable as Bristol East was a radical centre of Labour agitation for many years.

A joint appeal in September 1936 signed by representatives of the Labour League of Youth, Young Communist League and Co-operative Comrades Circle appealed for a joint campaign for the defence of democracy in Spain – and so an Aid for Spain committee was formed with Bill Nicholas as secretary.

Propaganda in support of the young Spanish Republic was organized and collections taken, particularly for food. Massive regular Sunday night meetings with national speakers were held at the Old Empire and Olympia theatres in Bristol – both of which were owned by Labour sympathizers. Weekend street meetings and collections were held regularly. At the city's largest factories, including Frys and Wills, regular collections were held on pay-days for an ambulance for Spain which the campaign bought in August 1937.

The unveiling ceremony, like those elsewhere in Britain, helped to bring together former comrades. Winifred Sandford was able to chat with Jack Jones about old times – they had known each other out in Spain.

Winifred Sandford (Bates) in Madrid, by the side of an ambulance just delivered from England.

MSF Divisional Office, Bristol

Bristol

ornwall conjures up tourism and holidays on sunny stretches of golden sands, Atlantic rollers, surfing and artists' colonies. But there is another Cornwall – one with a very strong, radical tradition, a Cornwall of tin mines and china clay workings, of fishermen and of unemployment and poverty. It did not escape from the depression of the 1930s and many Cornishmen became regular soldiers because there were few other avenues for providing for the family. Travelling fairs, boxing booths and wrestling were also means of putting a few shillings in one's pockets.

Patrick (called Harry by the family) Glasson was a Cornishman from Redruth, and it is not strange that with such a background he found himself fighting alongside Spanish workers for their liberty. He was for many years until 1935, a regular soldier serving in the Wiltshire Regiment. He had a sad childhood coming from a broken family background – his father having emigrated to Australia in 1912. His mother (née Byrne) was born in Ireland and Pat Glasson preferred to be identified with Ireland rather than Cornwall.

According to his cousin Reuben Byrne, also a regular soldier whom he met in 1935 at Crownhill Barracks, Plymouth, after a few months back in Redruth, Pat Glasson decided to join the International Brigade and went off to Paris. From Paris he wrote to his cousin Reuben on 17 April 1937:

> Just a few lines hoping to find you in the best of health. I am going away for sometime, and I don't know when I will be back in England. Well old boy I am joining an army but not the British army, it is the Spanish. I am fighting for the workers. I don't know when I will write again. Give my love to cousin Kathleen and Auntie Minnie and Uncle Jack at Truro. I might get married out here if all goes well in the end. I am your ever loving cousin Harry. P.S. I was wrestling in Paris the other day at a fair ground. I beat a giant Italian in a minute.

He also sent a card 'To Auntie Beatie' saying: 'This is what I am fighting for these Spanish workers.' On the reverse side the card showed a woman holding a child in her arms with silhouettes of planes above and an inscription in French: 'Save my child.'

In August 1937 his relations received letters from Communist Party general secretary Harry Pollitt and from the Party secretariat informing them that Pat Glasson had been killed in action on 20 July at Brunete. Later his Aunt Beattie received his death certificate signed by the Mayor of Brunete.

Pat Glasson's name is inscribed alongside those of eight other volunteers from Bristol and the South-West 'who fought and died in Spain in defence of Liberty' on a beautifully designed simple bronze plaque, which was unveiled at the Technical, Administrative and Supervisory Section of the AUEW (now the Manufacturing Science Finance Union) divisional office in Coldharbour Road, Redland, Bristol in July 1986.

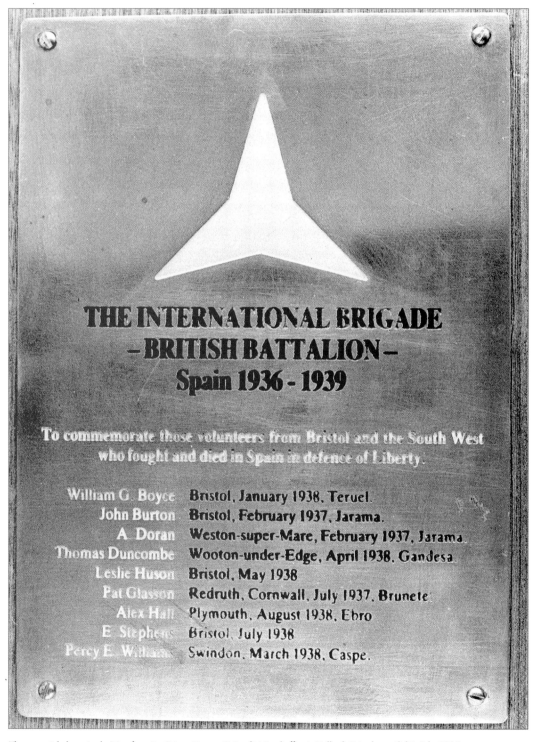

The memorial plaque in the Manufacturing Science Finance Union divisional office in Redland, Bristol, unveiled in July 1986.

The ceremony was organized by the then TASS divisional organizers D. Yeomans and D. Perkins and took place with a number of International Brigade veterans present.

The commemorative plaque honours those like Julian Bell, who gave up his pleasant life as professor of English at a Chinese university to go to Spain, because as he explained to the novelist E.M. Forster: 'Non-resistance means suffering the full power of fascism. And fascism means not only violence, but slavery, and will not only kill and torture, but will destroy all chances of reasonable or Christian opposition . . . and will do its best, with violence and propaganda, to harry out of the world all liberal and humane ideas and men.'

Julian Bell was killed driving an ambulance in the battle at Brunete.

A letter sent to Reuben Byrne by Harry Glasson from Paris and the message on the back of a postcard from him to 'Auntie Beatie'.

Whitworth Road Cemetery, Swindon

A young man, smart in his officer's white uniform and peaked cap standing on the deck of a ship bathed in sunlight looks out from the photograph with a serious expression on his youthful face. He is junior engineer Percy Williams – life stretches before him with all its promise.

He selflessly sacrificed that future at the age of twenty-two in the noble cause of fighting in the ranks of the British Battalion in solidarity with the Spanish people against fascism. He was killed in 1938 at the battle of Caspe, just two months after he had joined the International Brigade.

Bill Alexander in his book, *British Volunteers for Liberty*, describes how the British forces 'were forced to retreat through Caspe under intense and short-range rifle and machine gun fire. . . . The defence of Caspe, by a few hundred exhausted, poorly-armed men of the 15th Brigade, had broken

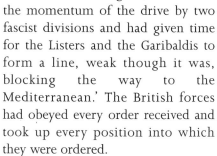

Junior Engineer Percy Williams on the ship's deck.

the momentum of the drive by two fascist divisions and had given time for the Listers and the Garibaldis to form a line, weak though it was, blocking the way to the Mediterranean.' The British forces had obeyed every order received and took up every position into which they were ordered.

Percy Williams, before going to sea, had been a member of the Swindon branch of the engineering union, having been a time-served apprentice at the town's Great Western rail works. In April 1939 the Swindon Amalgamated Engineering Union 2nd branch asked its district committee to 'devise some scheme by which the death of the late Bro P Williams who fought for the Liberty of Democracy and Trade Unions in Spain can be commemorated'. A month later the district committee agreed to erect a memorial in Whitworth Road Cemetery, calling on all branches and shop stewards to give their support. At the November district committee it was noted that the memorial had been erected.

In the March of the fiftieth anniversary year of the outbreak of the fascist rebellion against the young

Spanish Republic, members of the AEU district committee and friends gathered at the memorial in the cemetery when a wreath was laid in tribute to Percy Williams.

The following November, Thamesdown Borough Council decided to honour Percy Williams' memory by planting a Spanish chestnut tree at the local park, Coate Water. The tree was planted by Dick Pearce, past president of Swindon District AEU, at a ceremony attended by Thamesdown Borough Council leader Arthur Miles, when the International Brigade banner was unfurled by Bill Alexander and Max Colin of the International Brigade Association.

Another former apprentice at the same Swindon rail works was Ralph Bates, the author whose book about Spanish rural life, *The Olive Field*, first published on the eve of Franco's uprising, was republished in 1986. Ralph Bates worked in Spain at the docks in Barcelona, later living mainly in the Pyrenees. It was his mountaineering skills that enabled him to organize mountain scout troops against Franco. He edited the publication of the International Brigades – *Volunteer for Liberty* – and served at the front and on the staff at the defence of Madrid. His first wife Winifred helped to organize the medical volunteers.

The memorial to Percy Williams in Whitworth Road Cemetery, Swindon, erected in 1939 by the District Committee of the Amalgamated Engineering Union.

SOGAT Convalescent Home, Rottingdean

Rottingdean

Print workers not only have a long tradition of militancy in defence of their trade union rights, but also of the struggle against fascism. Soon after Hitler came to power the Printers' Anti-Fascist Movement was formed and it published *Anti-Fascist Printer*. So it was only natural that when the young Spanish Republic came under attack from Franco, print workers were in the forefront in showing their solidarity. On one occasion print workers marched along Fleet Street in protest at a pro-Franco article in *The Times*.

Their anti-fascist organization had its own Aid Spain Committee with delegates from five London printing works. By March 1938 £600 had been raised for the dependants of International Brigaders and by May the amount had increased to over £1,000. The *Anti-Fascist* carried regular reports from two print union members at the front in Spain – Bill Alexander and Lou Kenton. Figures published monthly showed regular collections among print workers in Manchester and London. The Society of Lithographic Artists, Designers and Engravers (SLADE), with only 7,500 members, collected £1,100 in 12 months, while the London Central Branch of the Paperworkers collected £900, and by July 1938 the Aid Spain Committee at Odhams Press received £1,062 for the dependants of volunteers. The *Daily Herald*, which was printed at Odhams, held weekly collections for the dependants. By the beginning of 1939 the Printers' Aid Committee had collected sufficient money to send a truck to Perpignan, full of drugs, medical equipment and food for Spanish refugees fleeing from Barcelona. After a big send-off from Fleet Street, the truck was taken out by Lou Kenton and two London Machine Branch members, who distributed their supplies and then ferried women, children and old people to what was hoped would be the safety of the French border.

Lou Kenton had gone to Spain in 1936 with paperworker George Hardy, who was employed by the *Daily Worker*, for the Barcelona Workers' Olympic Games, which had to be abandoned because of the Franco-led uprising. Both joined the International Brigade, Lou Kenton driving an ambulance, attached to one of the British hospitals in Spain, which had been sent by SLADE. George Hardy, a member of the Printing Machine branch of the National Union of Printing Bookbinders and Paper Workers and cyclist member of the National Workers Sports Association, was killed in the bloody fighting at Aragon in April 1938.

Another print worker and circulation manager of the *Daily Worker*, Wally Tapsell, fought in the International Brigade. He had joined the Communist Party at the age of sixteen and became a leader of the Young Communist

George Hardy, member of the Print Machine branch of SOGAT.

League. He went to Spain in February 1937 at the age of thirty-three. An experienced political leader, he was sent to Barcelona from Albacete to try to extricate members of the Independent Labour Party who had linked up with the Trotsky-influenced Partido Obrero de Unificación Marxista (POUM), some members of which in May 1937 had been fighting republican forces in the streets of the city. He became the battalion commissar and gave outstanding and inspirational leadership to his fellow volunteers in battle, and was commended for his leadership in the field. He was last seen alive firing his pistol at a fascist tank commander at Calaceite in April 1938.

Walter Tapsell (with cap) distributing food at the front.

A memorial plaque to George Hardy, Leslie Maugham, Walter Tapsell and Ralph Fox, all killed in Spain, has been placed on the terrace wall at the Society of Graphical and Allied Trades (SOGAT) Convalescent Home in Rottingdean, Sussex. A re-dedication of the plaque took place on 31 August 1986 with the then SOGAT general secretary, Brenda Dean, and the union's TUC delegates welcoming a number of International Brigade veterans.

The memorial plaque on the terrace wall at the SOGAT Convalescent Home in Rottingdean, Sussex, which was re-dedicated on 31 August 1986.

THIS TERRACE IS DEDICATED TO THE MEMORY OF FOUR GRAPHICAL WORKERS WHO WERE KILLED FIGHTING FASCISM IN SPAIN 1936-39

GEORGE HARDY - Printing Machine Branch, SOGAT
LESLIE MAUGHAM - London Machine Branch, SOGAT
WALTER TAPSELL - London Central Branch, SOGAT
RALPH FOX - London Branch, National Union of Journalists

Carved Boxes, St Albans

St Albans

Jim Ruskin.

The political transformation from a teenage interpreter for the British Army intervening against the young Soviet Republic in the Caucasus, to a volunteer in the International Brigade aiding the young Spanish Republic in its unequal struggle against Franco aided by Hitler and Mussolini, must be unique. But that is the story of Dovmont Sergeevich Zubchaninov or Jim Ruskin, as he was known in Britain, a linguist who spoke eight languages, who in 1923 joined the French Communist Party and later the British Communist Party.

He joined the International Brigade in 1936 and had a responsibility which called for exceptional skills, cool-headedness and utmost bravery. He commanded the transmissions department of the Brigade – laying field telephone lines in battle, maintaining them, carrying out repairs, making alternative lines, and no matter how fiercely the battle raged, headquarters and the front line had to be in continuous communication. Bill Rust in his book *Britons in Spain* says Jim Ruskin 'earned a great reputation for coolness under fire during the battle of Jarama'.

He was highly esteemed by the World Peace Council in Vienna for his skill as a translator and interpreter. He worked at the Pugwash meetings and at many scientific and other international conferences. He was a member of the St Albans branch of the Communist Party for many years and died in March 1990. At his funeral, his lifelong friend Claude Luxembourg called him a 'remarkable man' with a 'remarkable life'.

Another volunteer from the area was Tommy Hughes, also a member of the St Albans branch of the Communist Party. He lost a leg in the fighting in Spain. He hailed originally from Cambuslang, near Glasgow. Deteriorating health forced him to leave the Electrolux factory in Luton. He decided to become a chiropodist, and it was Tommy Hughes who treated the blisters of the footsore participants in the 1983 People's March for Jobs at the roadside, before they went on their final leg of the march to Westminster.

In 1982 the St Albans Communist Party branch decided to mark in some tangible form the contribution to the struggle for democracy and liberty of Jim Ruskin and his fellow anti-fascist, Tommy Hughes.

Dee Rogers, a very fine calligrapher and printmaker, was asked to make commemorative illuminated scrolls for each of the volunteers and sculptor Frank Casey to carve boxes to contain the scrolls. The boxes were made by disadvantaged youth in an inner-city project with which a member of the St Albans Communist Party branch, Syd Fogarty, a carpenter, was involved.

A commemoration event followed in a room at The Goat public house in St Albans. So many attended that people were compelled to stand outside on the pavement and in the pub's garden. Music was played and the poetry of C. Day Lewis, John Cornford and Charles Donnelly was recited. Following this the scrolls and carved boxes were presented to Jim Ruskin and Tommy Hughes.

The carved memorial box bearing Jim Ruskin's name —
a twin box to that bearing the name of Tommy Hughes,
both carved by Frank Casey, each containing an
illuminated scroll (top) made by Dee Rogers.

Banners

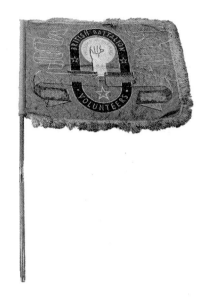

Only you can hear and see, behind the eyes of the sleepers, the movements and countries and tunes and wishes and flight and fall and despairs and big seas of their dreams.

Dylan Thomas

They sleep on Spanish soil or in their native lands. They marched and fought behind banners proudly held that proclaimed their defiance and determination to defend democracy – banners that are lowered only in homage to their courage and sacrifice – banners that today not only serve as poignant links to those past battles, but inspire the striving for liberty in those that follow. Such are the banners that have blazoned on them the battle honours of the British volunteers who fought with the International Brigade.

The first known was one identifying the small British group of about 100 after their return from the unsuccessful invasion of Majorca in August 1936. It is not known who made the banner, but it was photographed in September 1936 outside the Karl Marx Barracks in Barcelona with some of the volunteers. The inscription, probably by their leader Nat Cohen, read:

Centuria Inglesa Anti Fascista – Tom Mann – Disciplina Proletaria Anti Fascista Cera Al Fascismo
(The English Anti-fascist Centuria – Tom Mann – Proletarian anti-fascist discipline will stop fascism)

The first banner of the British Battalion was made by the Artists International Association (AIA) and presented to the battalion at Christmas 1937, at Mas de las Matas, Aragon. The AIA was closely bound up with the anti-fascist war in Spain. Its founders included Pearl Binder, Misha Black, James Boswell, James Fitton, James Lucas and Cliff Rowe. It was born out of the social and political conflicts of the early thirties and provided an unbroken link between the anti-fascist movement of the thirties and the cold war of the late forties and early fifties. By 1971 it had lost its original radicalism, changing increasingly to an artist-run exhibiting society.

Its first publication was of drawings of Hunger Marchers and its first exhibition, in 1934, was entitled *The Social Scene*. The second exhibition, *Artists Against Fascism and War*, coincided with the Italian fascist invasion of Abyssinia in 1935, the year which saw the publication of *5 on Revolutionary Art*, a collection of essays by Alick West, A.L. Lloyd, Francis Klingender, Eric Gill and Herbert Read. The AIA organized various fund-raising schemes throughout the anti-fascist war in Spain.

Among International Brigade members associated with the AIA were M.A. Rowley (Maro) who drew cartoons for the *Daily Worker* and Christopher Caudwell, both of whom were killed in Spain. Clive Branson and Hugh Slater, both of whom had connections with the AIA, also fought in Spain.

Opposite: Members of the Tom Mann Centuria with their banner outside the Karl Marx Barracks in Barcelona, September 1936. Left to right: Sid Avner, Nat Cohen, Ramona, Tom Wintringham, George Tioli, Jack Barry, Dave Marshall.

Harry Pollitt carrying the British Battalion banner made by the Artists International Association, near Teruel, Christmas 1937.

The British Battalion banner made by the AIA was designed by James Lucas and embroidered by Phyllis Ladyman. The shiny metal clenched fist on top of the banner pole was sculpted by Betty Rea. The banner was taken to Spain by the Communist Party general secretary Harry Pollitt, Professor J.B.S. Haldane and Bill Rust. It was with the battalion in the fighting on the Teruel front, but was lost, probably in the fascist breakthrough in March and April 1938. A replacement, using the same design, on which women in London worked through the night to complete, was speedily sent out to Spain and was brought back to Britain when all the International Brigades were withdrawn from Spain.

The banner headed protest marches and demonstrations outside the Spanish Embassy in Grosvenor Square during Franco's regime and his vicious terror against the Spanish people. Today, rather tattered by age and use, it is often paraded at funerals of International Brigaders.

On 7 October 1994 the banner was lowered on the battlefield of Jarama when a group of British Brigaders and families remembered the 161 British volunteers who fell in February 1937 in the successful defence of Madrid. Then the banner led the march into the cemetery at Morata de Tajuna where Spanish and international fighters are remembered.

When Major Clement Attlee MP, leader of the Labour Party, visited the British Battalion in December 1937 at Mondejar he agreed that the No. 1 Company be named after him. A banner bearing his name was made for the company. It was carried at the head of the Battalion when it marched while preparing for the assault across the Ebro. There is no record of what happened to the banner.

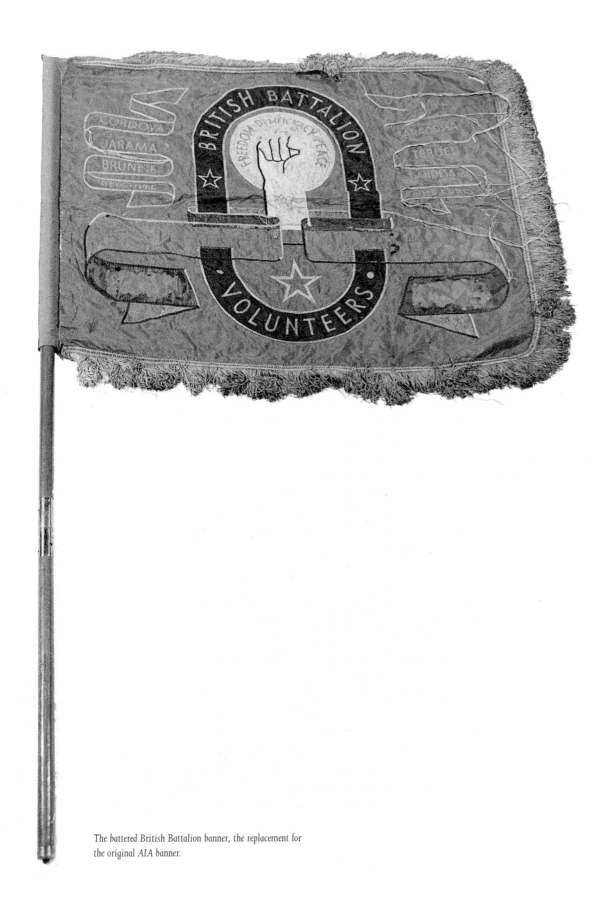

The battered British Battalion banner, the replacement for
the original *AIA* banner.

The Major Attlee Company banner displayed by members of the company with (right) company commander 'Taffy' Evans holding the banner.

Scottish, Welsh, English and Irish members of the British Battalion showing their Saklatvala ensign in Spain. Saklatvala was a Member of Parliament in the 1920s and had the distinction of being the first Communist to be elected to the House of Commons.

A beautiful banner, recording on a red background all the actions of British units from the defence of Madrid in November 1936 to the very last battle in the Sierra Caballs in September 1938, was made by the women of Barcelona. They were probably factory workers who were inspired by the role of the British volunteers. It was brought back to Britain, cleaned, mounted in a glazed frame and is today preserved and on display in the Marx Memorial Library, Clerkenwell Green, London, forming a colourful part of the International Brigade Archive.

The Scottish area of the National Union of Mineworkers commissioned and presented to the Scottish Brigaders a replica of the original Battalion banner but with wording specifically relating to the Scottish contribution to the anti-fascist war in Spain. The banner is in the People's Palace, Glasgow as a fitting memorial to the 437 volunteers who went out to Spain from Scotland.

Members of the British Battalion hold high the colourful banner made and presented to them by the women of Barcelona as they take part in the farewell parade in the city.

Mick McGahey, president of the Scottish National Union of Mineworkers presenting the Scottish International Brigade banner to veteran volunteers from Scotland. Phil Gillan is seen here receiving the banner and behind him is Peter Kerrigan.

Fuencarral

Many of the British, along with other International Brigaders killed in the fighting in and around Madrid, were buried in the Cemetery of Fuencarral, then a small village on the northern outskirts of Madrid. The high-walled cemetery, standing on a hill, contained the graves of local people. The Brigaders were buried in a special area marked by a simple plaque. Each grave was marked by a name on a wooden cross. With Franco's victory all traces of the graves were destroyed. After his death, with moves towards democracy, the Madrid city council placed a large marble plaque on an inside wall of the cemetery honouring the fallen International Brigaders. At the unveiling ceremony International Brigader Jim Jump spoke of the British fallen.

Jarama

After the four days of bloody and decisive battle to save Madrid, the British Battalion built a small cairn of rocks in the olive groves. It bore a wooden plaque inscribed with the names of the fallen. A guard of honour was mounted there on special occasions. Only after the fall of Madrid in March 1939 were the Franco forces able to walk across the battle front and destroy the memorial. Many British had been left behind the fascist lines or buried in shallow graves in the olive groves. When later cultivation exposed the remains of all those who had fallen they were taken to the village cemetery of Morata de Tajuna and dumped in an unmarked pit. Only after many years of enquiry and negotiation was it possible for the Madrid Regional Authority to erect a memorial in the cemetery. The inscription reads: 'To the memory of the Heroic Anti-Fascist Fighters of Spain and the International Brigades who in the Battle of Jarama gave their lives for the Liberty of Spain, Europe and the World.'

In October 1994 a party of fifty Brigadiers, families and friends from Britain and Ireland took part in the unveiling ceremony.

The memorial plaque on the inner wall of the cemetery at Fuencarral. The inscription in French reads:

Volunteers of the International Brigades
Fell as Heroes
For the Liberty of the Spanish People
For the Future Well-Being and Progress of Humanity

Colour party at the site of the Jarama memorial.

Brunete

The Brunete offensive made an initial advance at heavy cost. Franco, by concentrating his artillery on the surrounding heights and dominating the skies with German and Italian planes, was able to check and then drive back the Republican forces to their starting point. The advance and then retreat meant that some casualties were left, while others were buried where they fell – made possible by the light sandy soil. The legendary George Nathan of the 15th Brigade staff was hit in a bombing raid and died in hospital. He was given a military funeral and buried in the woods of Torrelodones. The graves of the sixty-two casualties of the Brunete offensive remain unmarked.

The original memorial stone tablet and wooden cross in front erected in memory of those who fell in the Battle of Jarama.

The memorial erected by the Madrid Regional Authority in the village cemetery of Morata de Tajuna.

Teruel

The British Battalion suffered heavy losses as they moved from their reserve position on the top of Santa Barbara down the cliff face and across the River Alfambra in clear view of the enemy whose artillery was firing over open sights. There were more losses as Franco's infantry forced a retreat into a tight arc round the command post and the river and cliff. Only a few casualties could be reached to be buried on the plateau behind the machine guns. At night, a small group of friends of the fallen, together with Charlotte Haldane, secretary of the Dependants' Aid Committee, went up to the plateau, where gathering round a wooden plaque bearing the names of the fallen, remembered and paid tribute to their comrades. The 'Valley of Jarama' had to be sung quietly since the enemy was only a few hundred yards away. There was no sign of the memorial and graves when a visit was made there in 1981.

The Ebro Crossing

The British Battalion fought their way from the Ebro River crossing and suffered heavy losses in the repeated but unsuccessful attacks to take Hill 481, the key to Gandesa and to the whole advance. They were then sent to hold Hill 666 on the Sierra Pandols against a two-battalion-strong fascist attack. Enemy control of this 2,200 ft hill would have given them domination of all the river crossings. The Battalion held their positions and were congratulated by the 15th Army Corps. Percy Ludwick, a London-born Soviet citizen, who commanded the fortification engineering company, built a memorial to the British and all the International Brigaders who fell in the Sierra Pandols. High up on this remote and barren mountain it escaped destruction by the fascists.

George Nathan (with pipe).

High up on Hill 666 the memorial built of slabs of concrete by Percy Ludwick and his sappers, dedicated to the British and all the International Brigaders who fell in the Sierra Pandols.

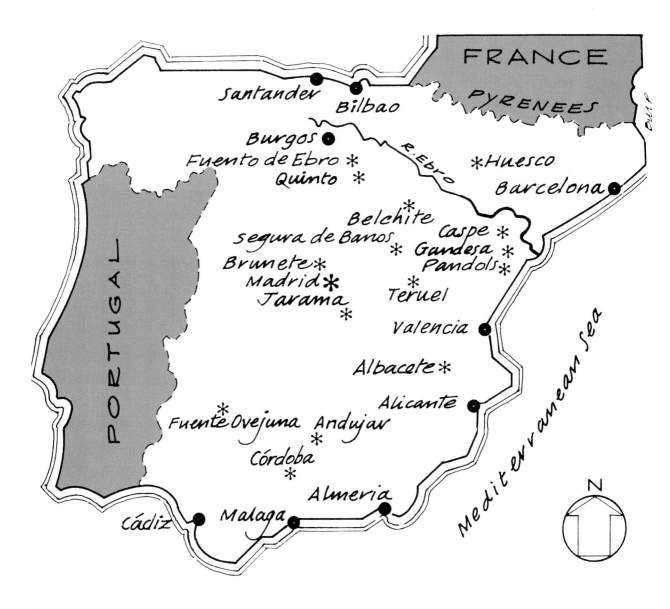

Key
* Principal places where the Battalion was in action
• Other major cities

Map of Spain showing the historic sites where the
British Battalion engaged in major battles.

Where Did They Die?

The Roll of Honour lists 526 names of volunteers who did not return to their families – they now rest in the rocks and soil of Spain.

Today their families – widows, children and grandchildren – want to learn more about the precise circumstances of the death of their loved ones and where they died. Their names may be inscribed on a memorial somewhere in Britain but people want more information to fill in the gaps in their knowledge. It is, however, almost impossible in every case to satisfy such natural requests, especially after the lapse of sixty years.

Maintaining accurate records of names, units, ranks and whereabouts of individuals was a difficult task in view of the fact that the International Brigade was part of the Republican Army, which itself had to be organized from scratch. Added to this was the pressure of having to face the overwhelming power of Franco's forces and their advance. There were the further complications of differences in spelling of names and alphabet coupled with the constant movement of individual volunteers.

With the formal integration of the International Brigade into the Republican Army on 12 October 1936, the establishing of their base in Albacete and the formation of the British Battalion on 31 January 1937, records and information became organized.

In the British Battalion, Ted Edwards and then Bob Cooney took great pains to keep track of volunteers and then to communicate information about the seriously wounded and those killed to their families.

There were mistakes and nearly always delays in keeping dependants and relatives in touch. This problem often caused concern and distress. Sometimes the correction of wrong information brought happiness. Tom Jones, a miner from Rhosllannerchrugog, North Wales was severely wounded in the Ebro offensive in September 1938. He was reported dead, his parents received his death certificate and a memorial meeting was held in Bangor. In fact he had been taken prisoner and only returned home in March 1940.

It was not only in battles and skirmishes that volunteers died. Some died as a result of accidents on land; some drowned when the SS *City of Barcelona*, taking them to Spain, was torpedoed; others died in hospital from wounds, illness and sheer physical exhaustion.

The British Battalion was in almost continuous action, moving from front to front, and two-thirds of its casualties fell in five major actions: twenty on the Madrid front, one hundred and sixty-one at Jarama, sixty-two at Brunete, twenty-four at Teruel and ninety-four in the Ebro offensive.

The First Few British in the Defence of Madrid

When the generals began their revolt against the legally elected Republican Government on 18 July 1936, there was initially little understanding in Britain of its full significance and the menace it presented. The Spanish people got hold of arms and with great heroism defeated reaction in five

of the main cities. But the realization spread that fascism could be victorious when German planes ferried Franco's mercenary Army of Africa into Spain, and that it could become yet another fascist state like Italy and Germany. Young anti-fascists in Britain, feeling they could no longer stand aside, decided to go to fight alongside the Spanish people. Many middle-class intellectuals, because they were already in possession of passports and experienced in travel, were among the first groups of British volunteers.

At Albacete a small group of British volunteers had attached themselves to the mainly French-speaking 11th International Brigade. Unknown to each other, another British group linked up with the mainly German-speaking 12th Brigade. The 11th went into action on 9 November 1936 when Franco's army had reached the outskirts of Madrid. Together with units of the newly-organized Republican army and civilians, they stopped the fascist advance in the streets of the Spanish capital. The British groups fought in University City while the fascists held other buildings a hundreds yards away. Then the 11th Brigade moved to meet threats at Aravaca, and stopped a fascist attack at Boadilla. By now deaths, wounds and illness had reduced the British group in the 11th Brigade to only five. The other British group, now numbering eighteen, went into action with the Thaelmans Brigade on 12 November. It suffered appalling losses in halting a fascist advance at Boadilla. By 20 December only two of this British group were still in action. After two months of fighting only five of the combined original thirty British 'first few' were fit for active service. Their courage, conviction and sacrifice had helped to save Madrid – the capital never fell to military assault and resisted fascism until 28 March 1939. These first British volunteers earned the highest reputation; they had been hardened in battle and learned to be disciplined. When they joined the British Battalion forming up in Madrigueras, they provided an invaluable reinforcement.

The Battle of Jarama

Beaten in his attempt to take Madrid by frontal assault, Franco commenced an encircling move aimed at cutting the only road from Madrid to the rest of Republican Spain. He concentrated a powerful force of 40,000 men, including the well-equipped Army of Africa, regular German machine gunners, tanks and artillery backed by strong air support. On 11 February 1937, having met with little resistance, this force crossed the Jarama River, the only natural obstacle before the Valencia road. Faced with this grim threat the Government brought in its best Spanish brigades and three International Brigades. The newly-formed British Battalion, as part of the 15th International Brigade, was rushed to the front. On 12 February, the 600 men, now equipped with new Soviet rifles but most without any battle experience, advanced towards the Jarama valley. Their task was to stop the fascist advance. They reached a hill – later dubbed 'Suicide Hill' – and ran into heavy enemy rifle and machine-gun fire. The Battalion fought bravely but suffered considerable losses in men and leaders. Tom Wintringham, the Battalion commander ordered a retreat back to the next ridge. The Moors, believing they faced no opposition, rushed over the hill. The Battalion's heavy machine guns, up to then silent because of wrong calibre ammunition, were now ready and took a very heavy toll, forcing the Moors back. The front held for seven hours.

During the night another Moorish unit had moved into the valley. At dawn, Harold Fry's machine guns opened fire at close range, inflicting very heavy losses and forcing the fascist remnants to seek safety behind Suicide Hill. However, on the right flank, the Dimitrov and Franco-Belge Battalions had been forced to retreat, which enabled the fascists to fire into the British flank. Taking advantage of the broken ground Franco's Foreign Legion infiltrated the Machine Gun Company positions, took prisoners and marched them off to the rear. That night the 160 left of the original 600 men organized defensive positions along a sunken road in the olive groves. There was only half a mile of flat plateau before the descent into the Tajuna valley and the key road. The next morning, on the third day of the battle, a fresh enemy brigade with tanks broke into the weak Battalion positions. Small groups, isolated and without any heavy weapons, moved back down the hill. Nothing stood between the fascist forces and the Valencia road. Jock Cunningham, who had taken command of the Battalion after Wintringham had been wounded, and Frank Ryan, an experienced Irish political leader, began to organize the groups of exhausted men. In the dusk they marched back up the hill towards the front they had left in the morning. They marched in step, singing the 'Internationale'. The fascists, thinking a new Republican unit had arrived, retreated. The British Battalion, all that was left of it, were back again holding the front. The Jarama front was never broken in action, the Republic could fight on for another two years. The losses had been severe – two-thirds of the Battalion had been captured or wounded, with 161 killed in the actions. In this battle the volunteers set the highest standards of bravery and determination.

The Battalion remained in the trenches without adequate leave until 17 June, possibly because only the best troops could stop a surprise attack and advance in the valley. It was here that Alex McDade wrote his satirical song 'There's a valley in Spain called Jarama'. Today in a different form it is sung at all ceremonies of the British International Brigade when they honour their fallen comrades and remember their anti-fascist pledges.

Brunete

The training and organization to form the army had continued. On 6 July 1937 the Government felt ready to launch an ambitious major offensive to relieve the threat to Madrid. The main force would move

from the foothills of the Sierra Guadarrama to the north of Madrid where another force would break out northwards from Villaverde to the south – the thrust northwards never took place. The British Battalion was one of the six in the reinforced 15th Brigade. An anti-tank battery of four Soviet-made guns manned by British volunteers gave additional punch. The northern force was to have bypassed any pockets of opposition and moved rapidly to take the high ground across the River Guadarrama. The concentration of troops and equipment went well but the plan began to go wrong from the first day. The plan to bypass the enemy-held villages was not followed and the crucial step to take the high ground, never achieved. The British Battalion suffered losses in a day and night engagement capturing the village of Villanueva de la Canada before moving unopposed towards the Mosquito Crest across the river. Franco immediately began to meet the threat, pouring in large reinforcements of his best troops. His artillery on the heights was able to pound all the Republican positions. The skies were full of German and Italian planes bombing even the smallest movement. Consequently supplies and food could only be brought in, and the wounded evacuated, after nightfall. There was a shortage of water. The Battalion attempted to reach Mosquito Crest but was driven back by the weight of fire and suffered heavy losses. Extreme conditions developed with no cover and soaring temperatures during the day. The Listers were finally driven out of Brunete by the powerful attacks. The British Battalion, which was reduced to 100 men, split into two groups, then faced encirclement and were forced to withdraw. The Anti-Tank Battery was able to fire at close range at Franco's troops which often attacked in groups. Finally on 25 July all the 15th Brigade was ordered to withdraw. Only forty-two men of the British Battalion staggered through Villanueva de la Canada where three hundred had gone into battle nineteen days before.

Teruel

On 17 December 1937 the Government, using only Spanish units, captured the town of Teruel. The 15th Brigade was moved from the Madrid sector in preparation to meet the inevitable counter-attacks. At first the British Battalion was based on the flank of the salient on the 3,500 ft high Sierra Palomera. The cold was extreme with temperatures dropping to -20°C on some nights. Snow was everywhere with drifts two or three feet deep. The fascist planes had control of the air which meant the volunteers had to be out in the open in the trenches during the day, only being able to retire to the abandoned buildings under cover of darkness. The Battalion suffered from cold and frostbite though casualties were light. Being checked in their attempts to break out of the salient, the fascists mobilized 600 guns and an immense air fleet and tried to recapture Teruel by frontal assault. At first the Battalion was held in reserve, though machine guns were superbly positioned at the top of a cliff to fire on much of the front. The Thaelmanns and Marineros on the flanks were forced to retreat, leaving the front exposed. Then the rifle companies were ordered down the cliff face across the Alfambra river to take up the 'Post of Honour' position with the their backs to the river and cliff. Next day fascist artillery plastered the whole front at point blank range. A withdrawal had to be made with new positions only 100 yards from the river command post. The following day a concentrated attack by enemy infantry and cavalry was repulsed and the attempt to retake Teruel by frontal assault was abandoned. The battalion was then sent about forty miles north to Segura de los Banos to attack a road junction and so ease the pressure on Teruel. This was the final action on the Teruel sector.

Ebro Offensive

In April 1938 Franco's forces had broken through and reached the sea. Republican Spain was divided into two with the River Ebro being the effective boundary with Catalonia. Franco then moved his offensive southwards towards Valencia, his aim being to encircle Madrid and the central front. Spanish Prime Minister Negrin, wanting to relieve the pressure on that front and possibly end the division of the country, prepared to launch an offensive across the wide, fast-flowing Ebro. It was carefully planned with special training. The 15th Brigade with the British Battalion, heavily reinforced with Spanish troops, went across the river in boats on 25 July. Their orders were to push inland towards Corbera and Gandesa. This they successfully accomplished and took prisoners. But already the fascists, seeing the threat, brought up artillery and men while their planes bombed the river crossings incessantly. The next day the Battalion was ordered to take Hill 481. It was heavily fortified with barbed wire, trenches and bunkers. It was the key to Gandesa, an important road junction, essential for the Republican advance. Their first attack was repulsed but the attacks continued for the next six days taking them to within grenade-throwing range. The defences were almost impregnable and the attackers were pounded by artillery from Gandesa. The last effort made on August Bank Holiday got to within a couple of yards of the objective, but the odds were too great. After a short rest but still under fire, the Battalion was relocated to defend Hill 666 on the Sierra Pandols. Then with further fascist advances threatening to cut the road to the river, the Battalion was recalled for what was to be their last battle. When they went into action on 23 September, the Battalion strength was three hundred and seventy-seven, of whom one hundred and six were British. When it was withdrawn on the night of

24 September, it was one hundred and seventy-three, of whom fifty-eight were British. Two hundred men had been killed, were missing or had been taken prisoner. But the Battalion held its position.

Prime Minister Negrin, for diplomatic reasons, ordered the withdrawal of all foreign fighters. That night the 15th Brigade, with the remnants of the British Battalion, left the front and moved back across the river.

Medal forged to mark the fiftieth anniversary by the Republican supporters in Madrid with the inscription in Spanish: For Peace, Democracy, Freedom.

ROLL
OF
HONOUR

M. Aaronberg, Sheffield, February 1937, Jarama
N. Abramson, London, April 1938, Gandesa
Harry Addley, Folkestone, December 1936, Boadilla
Frank Airlie, Newcastle upon Tyne, July 1938, Ebro
John Alexander, Dundee, July 1937, Brunete
G. Allstop, Rotherham, August 1938, Ebro
J. Alwyn, Bolton, February 1937, Jarama
Antonis Anastasius, London–Cyprus, March 1938, Caspe
Alexander Armstrong, Manchester, February 1937, Jarama
F. Ash, Glasgow, March 1938, Aragon
J. Atkinson, Hull, February 1937, Jarama
C. Avgherinos, London–Cyprus, April 1937, Jarama
Sidney Avner, London, December 1936, Boadilla

William Bailey, Harwood, Lancs, June 1937, Jarama
W. Ball, Reading, February 1937, Jarama
W. Banks, Manchester, March 1938, Ebro
William Barry, Dublin, December 1936, Boadilla
N. Baxter, Leeds, February 1937, Jarama
R. Beadles, Birkenhead, February 1937, Jarama
W. Beales, Newport, Isle of Wight, August 1938, Ebro
John W. Beaton, Glasgow, August 1938, Ebro
William Beattie, Belfast, July 1937, Brunete
Clem Beckett, Oldham, February 1937, Jarama
R. Beckett, London, July 1938, Ebro
Julian Bell, London, July 1937, Brunete
C.A. Bennett, Walsall, July 1938, Ebro
Albert Bentley, London, November 1936, Casa del Campo
J. Bentley, Hull, March 1938, Aragon
John Berry, Edinburgh, February 1937, Jarama
L. Bibby, London, February 1937, Jarama
Lorrimer Birch, London, December 1936, Boadilla
A.E. Bird, London, July 1937, Brunete
John Black, Dover, July 1937, Brunete
R.C. Blair, London, April 1938, Gandesa
W. Bogle, Liverpool, February, 1937, Jarama
R. Bolger, London, May 1937, Jarama
Henry Bonar, Dublin, December 1936, Córdoba
Hugh Bonar, Dungloe, Ireland, February 1937, Jarama
Kenneth P. Bond, London, July 1938, Ebro
Alex Bonner, Glasgow, February 1937, Jarama
H.T. Bosley, Stoke, July 1938, Ebro
Bruce Boswell, Coventry, July 1938, Ebro
William G. Boyce, Bristol, January 1938, Teruel
Dan Boyle, Belfast, July 1938, Ebro
Kenneth Bradbury, Oldham, January 1938, Teruel

Thomas Brannon, Blantyre, Scotland, February 1937, Jarama
S.A. Breedon, London, July 1938, Ebro
William Brent, Barnsley, March 1938, Ebro
Robert Bridges, Leith, February 1937, Jarama
George Bright, Thornbury-on-Tees, February 1937, Jarama
William Briskey, London, February 1937, Jarama
Clement Broadbent, Dewsbury, Yorks, September 1938, Ebro
Thomas Bromley, Southwick, Durham, April 1938, Gandesa
N. Brookfield, Maidstone, September 1938, Ebro
H.M. Brooks, London, July 1938, Ebro
Frank Brown, Prestwich, July 1938, Ebro
George Brown, Manchester, July 1937, Brunete
W. Brown, Stockport, killed, whereabouts unknown
W.J. Brown, Newmilns, Ayrshire, February 1937, Jarama
Felicia Browne, London, August 1936, Aragon
John Bruce, Alexandria, February 1937, Jarama
Dave Buffman, Leeds, September 1938, Ebro
E. Burke, London, February 1937, Córdoba
T. Burke, Glasgow, July 1937, Brunete
J.P. Burley, Stoke, March 1938, Ebro
J. Burton, Bristol, February 1937, Jarama
H. Byrom, Manchester, March 1938, Ebro

D. Cameron, Glasgow, February 1937, Jarama
J. Campbell, London, February 1937, Jarama
Ralph Campeau, London, February 1937, Jarama
Ahillea C. Canaris, London–Cyprus, July 1937, Brunete
Ralph Cantorovitch, Manchester, July 1937, Brunete
Phil Caplan, London, July 1937, Brunete
A. Capps, London, January 1938, Teruel
H. Carass, ?, killed, whereabouts unknown
Anthony Carritt, Oxford, July 1937, Brunete
T.J. Carter, West Hartlepool, February 1937, Jarama
James Cassidy, Glasgow, February 1937, Jarama
Payaniotis Catsaronas, London–Cyprus, February 1937, Jarama
P. Charlton, Leeds, February 1937, Jarama
W. Clasper, London, July 1938, Ebro
Lewis Clive, London, August 1938, Ebro
Denis Coady, Dublin, January 1937, Las Rozas
James Cockburn, London, January 1937, Córdoba
S. Codling, South Shields, March 1938, Caspe
William Coles, Cardiff, February 1937, Jarama
J. Connolly, Glasgow, February 1937, Jarama
Frank Conroy, Kildare, December 1936, Córdoba
Kit Conway, Tipperary, February 1937, Jarama
Jim Coomes, London, September 1937, Aragon

Charles E. Cormack, London, August 1938, Ebro
John Cornford, Cambridge, December 1936, Córdoba
G. Corry, Cleckheaton, Yorks, March 1938, Caspe
Robert Coutts, North Shields, February 1937, Jarama
M. Cox, Dundee, March 1938, Aragon
Ray Cox, Southampton, December 1936, Boadilla
William Cox, London, February 1937, Jarama
A. Craig, Glasgow, February 1937, Jarama
George Craig, Ulmanston, February 1937, Jarama
C.W. Cranfield, London, January 1938, Teruel
William J. Crawford, Glasgow, February 1937, Jarama
W.E. Crispin, London, April 1938, Gandesa
Fraser Crombie, Kirkcaldy, July 1937, Brunete
Ed Cross, London, April 1938, Gandesa
R. Cruickshanks, Glasgow, April 1938, Gandesa
Alec Cummings, Tonypandy, September 1938, Ebro
James Cunningham, Glasgow, August 1938, Ebro
Pat Curley, Dumbarton, February 1937, Jarama

J. Dalgish, Leigh, Lancs, February 1937, Jarama
Peter Daly, Enniscorthy, Ireland, September 1937, Quinto
M. Davidovitch, London, February 1937, Jarama
Thomas Davidson, Aberdeen, April 1937, Gandesa
Adam Davie, Glasgow, February 1937, Jarama
Harold Davies, Neath, February 1937, Jarama
William Davies, Dublin, July 1937, Brunete
William J. Davies, Tonypandy, July 1937, Brunete
G. Deegan, Balloch, Ireland, January 1938, Teruel
Vincent Deegan, Brighton, March 1938, Ebro
Archibald Dewar, Aberdeen, March 1938, Ebro
P. Dewhurst, Oxford, July 1937, Brunete
E.A. Dickinson, London, February 1937, Jarama, shot while prisoner
W.J. Dickson, Prestonpans, July 1937, Brunete
Harry Dobson, Rhondda, July 1938, Ebro
Walter Dobson, Leeds, August 1938, Ebro
Frank Docherty, Glasgow, July 1938, Ebro
John Dolan, Glasgow, February 1937, Jarama
Thomas Dolan, Sunderland, February 1937, Jarama
Charles Dolling, London, July 1937, Brunete
James Domegan, London, September 1938, Ebro
J. Donald, Methill, March 1938, Belchite
W. Donaldson, Glasgow, January 1938, Teruel
S. Donnell, Glasgow, April 1938, Calaceite
Charles Donnelly, Tyrone, February 1937, Jarama
A. Doran, Weston-super-Mare, February 1937, Jarama
J. Douglas, Glasgow, February 1937, Jarama

F. Drinkwater, Burnley, July 1937, Brunete
G.N. Drury Fuller, Maidstone, September 1938, Ebro
James Duffy, Glasgow, April 1938, Ebro
A. Dunbar, London, July 1937, Brunete
Richard Duncan, Tillicoultry, Scotland, September 1938, Flix
Thomas Duncombe, Wotton, Glos, April 1938, Gandesa
Martin Durkin, Middlesbrough, August 1938, Ebro
W.F. Durston, Aberaman, September 1938, Ebro

Sydney Edelman, London, April 1938, Aragon
Phillip Elias, Leeds, February 1937, Jarama, shot while prisoner
Robert S. Elliott, Blyth, Northumberland, July 1937, Brunete
Thomas Elliott, Worthing, June 1937, Jarama
Victoriano Esteban, Abercrave, South Wales, killed, whereabouts unknown
Edwin A. Evans, Glasgow, March 1938, Aragon

J. Fairchild, London, March 1938, Ebro
J. Fellingham, Bury, January 1938, Teruel
R. Felton, Rochester, February 1937, Jarama
John Ferguson, ?, killed, whereabouts unknown
Sydney Fink, Salford, March 1938, Aragon
A. Finnan, Dundee, March 1938, Belchite
H.D. Fisher, Romsey, Hants, July 1938, Ebro
Thomas Flecks, Blantyre, April 1937, Chimorra
J.F. Flynn, Glasgow, April 1937, Córdoba
Ralph Fox, Halifax, December 1936, Córdoba
Tony Fox, Dublin, December 1936, Córdoba
William Fox, Blantyre, February 1937, Jarama
C.L. Foxall, Sale, Cheshire, February 1937, Jarama
Archibald (Josh) Francis, Reading, March 1938, Aragon
S. Francis, London, January 1938, Teruel
F. Freedman, London, January 1938, Teruel
George Fretwell, Penygroes, North Wales, February 1937, Jarama
Harold Fry, Edinburgh, October 1937, Fuentes de Ebro

Michael Gallagher, Wigan, July 1937, Brunete
P. Garland, Glasgow, July 1938, Ebro
T. Gaunt, Chesterfield, March 1838, Aragon
W. Gauntlett, Glasgow, July 1938, Ebro
Thomas Gibbons, London, July 1937, Brunete
W.J. Giles, Liverpool, February 1937, Jarama
J. Gilmour, Prestonpans, February 1937, Jarama
Pat Glacken, Greenock, January 1938, Teruel
Ben Glaser, London, September 1938, Ebro
Pat Glasson, Redruth, Cornwall, July 1937, Brunete
R. Glen, Alexandria, July 1938, Ebro

A. Gold, London, February 1937, Jarama
H. Gomm, London, February 1937, Jarama
Charles Goodfellow, Bellshill, Scotland, July 1937, Brunete
Michael Goodison, Salford, April 1938, Ebro
R. Goodman, Nottingham, February 1937, Jarama
W.R. Goodman, Salford, February 1937, Jarama
George Gorman, Derry, September 1938, Ebro
William J. Gough, Luton, December 1936, Boadilla
R.A. Grant, London, March 1938, Calaceite
T. Grant, Nottingham, March 1938, Aragon
George Green, Stockport, September 1938, Ebro
Leo Green, Dublin, February 1937, Jarama
M. Green, Manchester, March 1938, Aragon
R. Grierson, Annan, March 1938, Aragon
Henry Gross, London, July 1937, Brunete
D. Grossart, Glasgow, April 1937, Jarama
E. Guerin, London, August 1937, Quinto
David Guest, London, July 1938, Ebro
Mark Gura, London, February 1937, Jarama

Alex Hall, Plymouth, August 1938, Ebro
John Hall, Rutherglen, March 1938, Belchite
David Halloran, Middlesbrough, February 1937, Jarama
T. Hamill, Glasgow, February 1937, Jarama
Sid Hamm, Cardiff, July 1937, Brunete
James Harding, Stockton-on-Tees, September 1938, Ebro
George Hardy, London, April 1938, Aragon
James Harkins, Clydebank, July 1938, Ebro
A. Harris, Liverpool, July 1937, Brunete
T.J. Harris, Llanelli, February 1937, Jarama
Alex Harvey, Glasgow, February 1937, Jarama
Martin Hempel, London, July 1938, Ebro
David Henderson, Glasgow, February 1937, Jarama
James Henderson, London, July 1937, Brunete
Richard Henderson, Kirkcaldy, April 1938, Ebro
William Henry, Belfast, February 1937, Jarama
Ivor Hickman, Petersfield, Hants, September 1938, Ebro
Robert M. Hilliard, Killarney, February 1937, Jarama
S. Hilton, Newhaven, July 1938, Ebro
Arnold Hoare, Leeds, August 1938, Ebro
Albert Hobbs, Chelmsford, September 1938, Ebro
G. Hollanby, Liverpool, April 1938, Gandesa
Roger Hone, Hammersmith, August 1938, Ebro
Dick Horradge, Swansea, July 1937, Brunete
J. Howarth, Manchester, July 1938, Ebro
William Hudson, Newcastle upon Tyne, October 1938, Chapineria

V.J. Hunt, London, July 1937, Brunete
W. Hunter, Glasgow, March 1938, Aragon
Leslie Huson, Bristol, May 1938, killed, whereabouts unknown
C. Hyman, Glasgow, March 1937, Jarama
James Hyndman, Glasgow, January 1937, Las Rozas

E. Jackman, Liverpool, February 1937, Jarama
George Jackson, Cowdenbeath, August 1938, Sierra Pandols
William Jackson, Oldham, April 1938, Gandesa
Sydney James, Treherbert, July 1938, Ebro
W.E. Jasper, London, February 1937, Jarama
Arnold Jeans, Manchester, December 1936, Boadilla
Wilf Jobling, Blaydon-on-Tyne, February 1937, Jarama
Thomas Johnson, London, July 1938, Ebro
W. Johnson, Newcastle upon Tyne, December 1936, Córdoba
D.E. Jones, London, July 1938, Ebro
D.J. Jones, Rhondda, February 1937, Jarama
E. Jones, ?, December 1936, Madrid
H. Fred Jones, London, November 1936, Madrid
James Jones, Harrow, July 1938, Ebro
T. Howell Jones, Aberdare, August 1938, Ebro
L. Jordan, Manchester, July 1937, Brunete
R.P. Jordan, Wembley, March 1938, Caspe
Emmanuel Julius, London, November 1936, Aragon

W. Keegan, Glasgow, July 1937, Brunete
F. Keery, ?, July 1938, Ebro
G. Kelly, Greenock, July 1939, Ebro
Michael Kelly, Ballinsaloe, Ireland, July 1937, Brunete
W. Kelter, Glasgow, March 1938, Gandesa
A. Kemp, Glasgow, January 1938, Teruel
W. Kenny, Manchester, February 1937, Jarama
J. Kent, New Zealand, June 1937, drowned when SS *City of Barcelona* sunk
J. Keogh, Ashton-under-Lyne, March 1938, Calaceite
James Kermode, Milngavie, Scotland, January 1937, Las Rozas
Thomas Kerr, Belfast, October 1938, died of typhoid in Vich hospital
A. Kerry, London, July 1937, Brunete
Frank Kerry, Gateshead, July 1938, Brunete
T.F. Killick, Southport, February 1937, Jarama
R. Kirk, Liverpool, February, 1937, Jarama
James Knottman, Manchester, January 1937, Córdoba
W. Knowles, London, February 1937, Jarama

Clifford Lacey, London, September 1938, Ebro
G. Lamb, London, April 1938, Gandesa
James Langham, Motherwell, July 1937, Brunete

W. Langmead, London, July 1937, Brunete
L.G. Large, London, April 1938, died as prisoner of war
C.A. Larlham, London, October 1937, Fuentes de Ebro
William Laughlin, Belfast, July 1937, Brunete
James Laughran, Motherwell, July 1937, Brunete
J. Lawrie, London, August 1938, Ebro
Harold Laws, Southampton, February 1938, Teruel
Clifford Lawther, Hexham, Northumberland, February 1937, Jarama
D.A. Ledbury, Swansea, July 1938, Ebro
Samuel Lee, London, February 1937, Jarama
Joseph Lees, Oldham, July 1937, Brunete
Alexander Leppard, London, February 1937, Jarama
G.S. Leslie, London, July 1937, Brunete
Ariel Levine, London, March 1938, Aragon
S. Lewis, London, July 1938, Ebro
A. Lichfield, London, July 1938, Ebro
M. Livesay, London, June 1937, Segovia
Sidney Lloyd Jones, Wales, October 1936, Chapineria
T.C. Loader, Bexley, Kent, December 1937, died of fever, whereabouts unknown
J. Lobban, Alexandria, September 1938, Ebro
R.K. Lomax, Shrewsbury, February 1937, Jarama
W.E. Lower, Sunderland, June 1937, drowned when SS *City of Barcelona* sunk
James Lyons, Glasgow, February 1937, Jarama

Albert McCabe, Bootle, Lancs, August 1937, Quinto
F. McCabe, Dundee, July 1937, Brunete
B. McCafferty, London, July 1938, Ebro
F. McCulloch, Glasgow, October 1937, Aragon
Alex McDade, Glasgow, July 1937, Brunete
Donald McDonald, Brighton, April 1938, Gandesa
R. McDonald, Glasgow, June 1937, drowned when SS *City of Barcelona* sunk
James McElroy, Wishaw, Scotland, April 1937, Jarama
G. McEwen, Liverpool, June 1937, Jarama
D. McGower, Glasgow, March 1938, Aragon
H. McGrath, Belfast, September 1938, Ebro
Alex McGregor, London, January 1938, Teruel
William S. McGregor, Dublin, September 1938, Ebro
Eamon McGrotty, Derry, February 1937, Jarama
E. McGuire, Dundee, February 1937, Jarama
W. McGuire, Dundee, February 1937, Jarama
James McHugh, Dundee, March 1938, Gandesa
David McKay, Milngavie, Scotland, April 1938, Gandesa
David McKay, Glasgow, August 1938, Ebro
McKenzie, Glasgow, March 1938, Aragon
A. McKeown, Glasgow, July 1937, Brunete
G. McKeown, Liverpool, June 1937, Jarama

Robert H. Mackie, Sunderland, July 1937, Brunete
William Mackie, London, August 1938, Ebro
J. McKissock, Glasgow, April 1937, Jarama
J. McLanders, Dundee, April 1937, Jarama
J. McLannaghan, Greenock, September 1938, Tarragona
F. McLaughlin, Newmains, Lanarkshire, killed, whereabouts unknown
G.C. McLaurin, Cambridge and New Zealand, November 1936, Madrid
Charles McLeod, Aberdeen, August 1938, Ebro
T. McLeod, Liverpool, March 1938, Aragon
Tim McManus, London, killed, whereabouts unknown
James McMorrow, Glasgow, July 1938, Ebro
W. McMullen, Belshill, Scotland, January 1938, Teruel
Arthur McNally, Birmingham, March 1938, Aragon
Thomas McWhirter, Glasgow, March 1938, Caspe
A. Madero, Louth, Lincs, April 1938, died in hospital
M. Mandell, London, July 1937, Brunete
A. Marks, London, July 1937, Brunete
Inver A.R. Marlow (John Scott), London, February 1937, Jarama
James Marshall, Clydebank, August 1938, Ebro
Bert Maskey, Manchester, February 1937, Jarama
N. Mason, Carshalton, Surrey, March 1938, Aragon
Robert Mason, Edinburgh, February 1937, Jarama
Sam Masters, London, July 1937, Brunete
H. Matthews, Cuffley, Herts, April 1938, Gandesa
Leslie Maugham, London, January 1938, Teruel
Michael May, Dublin, December 1936, Córdoba
John Meehan, Galway, December 1936, Córdoba
Cecil Mennel, London, January 1938, Teruel
William Meredith (Bob Dennison), Glasgow, July 1938, Brunete
Martin Messer, Glasgow, December 1936, Boadilla
George Middleton, Reading, November 1936, Casa de Campo
J. Miller, Glasgow, March 1938, Aragon
Morris Miller, Hull, August 1938, Ebro
James Moir, Perth, July 1937, Brunete
J.A. Moore, Portsmouth, January 1939, died of wounds
Thomas Moore, Manchester, January 1938, Teruel
Ken Morrice, Aberdeen, July 1938, Ebro
A. Morris, Cardigan, 1937, Madrid
William Morris, Llanelli, July 1937, Brunete
Phil Morriss, London, February 1937, Jarama
Sam Morriss, Ammanford, South Wales, July 1937, Brunete
Christos Mortakis, London–Cyprus, April 1938, Gandesa
R. Moss, London, April 1938, Gandesa
J.D. Mudie, Dundee, March 1938, Caspe
Alexander Muir, London, February 1937, Jarama
Dan Murphy, Cardiff, April 1938, Gandesa

James Murphy, Glasgow, March 1938, Caspe
Ben Murray, Belfast, March 1938, Aragon
James Murray, Glasgow, July 1937, Brunete
James Murray, Dundee, March 1938, Caspe
Joe Murray, London, March 1938, Aragon
William Murray, Glasgow, July 1937, Brunete

Jack Nalty, Dublin, September 1938, Ebro
Max Nash, London, July 1938, Ebro
George Nathan, London, July 1937, Brunete
J. Ness, Dundee, July 1938, Ebro
F. Newbury, Manchester, February 1937, Jarama
J. Newman, Liverpool, February 1937, Jarama
Arthur Newsome, Sheffield, January 1937, Córdoba
Demidrus Nicolaou, London–Cyprus, March 1938, Gandesa
Michael Nolan, Dublin, December 1936, Córdoba
J.T. Norbury, Liverpool, February 1937, Jarama
Frank Norton, Liverpool, February 1937, Jarama
M. Nuns (Emile Pezaro), London, March 1938, Aragon

Francis Duffy O'Brien, Dundalk, January 1938, Teruel
Thomas T. O'Brien, Liverpool, February 1937, Jarama
Peter O'Day, London, March 1938, Aragon
Tom Oldershaw, London, March 1938, Aragon
Dick O'Neill, Belfast, February 1937, Jarama
L. O'Nichen, Stoke, June 1938, Ebro
Loukas Orfanides, London–Cyprus, March 1938, Belchite
Ruth Ormesby, ?, April 1938, Barcelona
Paddy O'Sullivan, Dublin, July 1938, Ebro
Bert Overton, Stockton, July 1937, Brunete
Frank Owen, Mardy, South Wales, July 1937, Brunete
J.D. Owens, Liverpool, February 1937, Jarama

George Palmer, London, January 1937, Las Rozas
J. Palzeard, South Shields, February 1937, Jarama
Spiros Pantelides, London–Cyprus, March 1938, Belchite
Alec Park, Glasgow, March 1938, Aragon
A. Parkes, Manchester, July 1937, Brunete
Tom Patten, Dooega, Achill Isle, Co. Mayo, December 1936, Madrid
Edward Paul, London, February 1937, Jarama
Henry Pearson, London, July 1938, Ebro
Nikos Perdicos, London–Cyprus, February 1937, Jarama
Leonard Perry, London, April 1938, Gandesa
Arthur Perryman, London, April 1938, died in hospital
J. Peterson, Liverpool, April 1938, Gandesa
E. Petrie, London, August 1937, Brunete

Thomas Picton, Rhondda, April 1938, killed while prisoner
J. Pitman, London, April 1937, Chimorra
F.A. Plumb, Luton, February 1937, Jarama
A. Porter, Manchester, February 1937, Jarama
Frank J. Procter, Liverpool, August 1938, Ebro
Lawrence G. Pryme, London, August 1938, Ebro
A. Purvis, Edinburgh, April 1938, Gandesa

Maurice P. Quinlan, Waterford, Ireland, February 1937, Jarama
Frank Quinton, London, June 1937, Morata

James Rae, Glasgow, February 1937, Jarama
Harry Rawson (Heap), Oldham, December 1936, Córdoba
K. Rebbechi, Melbourne, Australia, January 1939, died in Vich hospital
J. Redhill, Glasgow, October 1937, Aragon
J. Redmond, Liverpool, March 1938, Aragon
Harry Reynolds, Newcastle, February 1937, Jarama
John Rickman, London, February 1937, Jarama
J. Riddell, Glasgow, October 1937, Aragon
John Riley, Glasgow, January 1938, Teruel
J.E. Riordan, London, April 1938, Ebro
J. Roach, Leeds, March 1938, Gandesa
Victor Robilliard, Dagenham, October 1938, Ebro
A. Leonard Robinson, Blackhall, Durham, October 1937, Fuentes de Ebro
Joseph C. Roche, Leeds, February 1937, Jarama
Roman Rodriguez, Dowlais, South Wales, July 1937, Brunete
John Ross, Edinburgh, March 1938, Aragon
George Rossides, London–Cyprus, April 1938, Gandesa
W.C. Rowney (Maro), London, February 1937, Jarama
James Rutherford, Edinburgh, April 1938, shot while prisoner
Maurice Ryan, Tipperary, August 1938, Ebro
Edward Ryder, London, June 1938, died of wounds while prisoner

D. Samson, Dundee, July 1937, Brunete
Alexander Scott, April 1937, Chimorra
C.J. Scott, London, August 1938, Ebro
H.G. Scott, London, February 1937, Jarama
James Scott, Swansea, March 1938, Caspe
William Seal, London, February 1937, Jarama
Nathan Segal, London, December 1936, Córdoba
Vic Shammah, Manchester, March 1938, Aragon
D. Sheehan, Brighton, July 1938, Ebro
Jack Sherpenzeel, London, July 1938, Ebro
B. Shields, Clydebank, March 1938, Caspe
J. Shields, Glasgow, February 1937, Jarama
R. Shields, Glasgow, September 1938, Ebro

Thomas Silcock, Liverpool, February 1937, Jarama
Ernest Sim, Aberdeen, September 1938, Ebro
C.J. Simmons, Portsmouth, February 1937, Jarama
A.C. Smith, Manchester, August 1938, killed while prisoner
David Smith, Glasgow, February 1937, Jarama
Harry J. Smith, Gateshead, February 1937, Jarama
John Smith, Irvine, Scotland, September 1938, Ebro
Malcolm Smith, Dundee, August 1938, Ebro
W. Smith, Birkenhead, March 1938, Aragon
Randall Sollenberger, London and USA, July 1937, Brunete
F. Spencer, Pontefract, February 1937, Jarama
Christopher St John Sprigg (Caudwell), London, February 1937, Jarama
Walter Sproston, Manchester, March 1938, Calaceite
Ken Stalker, London, February 1937, Jarama
John Steele, Falkirk, May 1937, Jarama
Nathan Steigman, London, February 1937, Jarama
T.E. Stephens, Bristol, July 1938, died in hospital
John Stevens, London, February 1937, Jarama, shot while prisoner
J.E. Stevens, London and Australia, July 1937, Brunete
Joseph Stevenson, Belshill, Scotland, February 1938, died of typhoid
Jim Stewart, Wallasey, February 1937, Jarama
George Stockdale, Leeds, July 1938, Ebro
Maurice Stott, Rochdale, February 1937, Jarama
James Straney, Belfast, July 1938, Ebro
Jim Strangward, Onllwyn, South Wales, August 1938, Ebro
L.R. Strickland, London, February 1937, Jarama
James Sullivan, Glasgow, July 1938, Ebro
Eddy Swindells, Manchester, February 1937, Jarama
Fred Sykes, Leicester, February 1937, Jarama
Jack Sylvester, London, February 1937, Jarama
Ronnie Symes, London, November 1936, Madrid

John Tadden, Dundee, February 1937, Jarama
H. Tagg, Doncaster, February 1937, Jarama
W. Tallis, London, April 1938, Gandesa
Louis Tanklevitch, Liverpool, July 1938, Ebro
Walter Tapsell, London, April 1938, Calaceite
Edward Tattam, Whitburn, Durham, March 1938, Aragon
William Tattam, Whitburn, Durham, July 1937, Brunete
G. Taylor, Cardiff, April 1938, Calaceite
J. Taylor, London, February 1937, Jarama
Terry ?, July 1937, Brunete
Brazell Thomas, Llanelli, July 1938, Ebro
J.G.C. Thomas, Gillingham, February 1937, Jarama
Andrew Thompson, Durham, January 1938, Teruel
Robert Traill, Cardiff, July 1937, Brunete

A. Trauber, London, September 1938, Ebro
Liam Tumilson, Belfast, February 1937, Jarama
F. Turnhill, Worksop, January 1938, Teruel

J. Unthank, Middlesbrough, February 1937, Jarama

Halcrow Verstage, London, July 1937, Brunete

J. Walsh, Liverpool, February 1937, Jarama
S.E. Walsh, Newcastle upon Tyne, July 1937, Brunete
Thomas Walsh, Dublin, February 1937, Jarama
David Walshe, Ballina, Ireland, January 1938, Teruel
F. Warbrick, London, March 1938, Aragon
R. Ward, Manchester, June 1937, Jarama
Robert Wardle, Hull, March 1938, Calaceite
J. Wark, Airdrie, February 1937, Jarama
J. Watson, Leicester, February 1937, Jarama
William Watson, Glasgow, July 1938, Ebro
James Watts, Swansea, August 1938, Ebro
Roy Watts, Leicester, September 1938, Ebro
W.A. Webb, London, February 1937, Jarama
G. Westfield, Liverpool, October 1937, Aragon
Eric Whalley, Mansfield, October 1937, Fuentes de Ebro
John Whalley, London, March 1938, Aragon
James Wheeler, London, February 1937, Jarama
Fred White, Ogmore Vale, South Wales, July 1937, Brunete
J. White, London, February 1937, Jarama
F. Whitehead, Manchester, February 1937, Jarama
Edgar Wilkinson, Sunderland, February 1937, Jarama
Norman Wilkinson, Manchester, February 1937, Jarama
Percy E. Williams, Swindon, March 1938, Caspe
J.E. Williams, Ammanford, South Wales, July 1937, Brunete
W. Williamson, London, July 1938, Ebro
Bernard Winfield, Nottingham, January 1938, Teruel
A. Winter, Glasgow, July 1937, Brunete
H. Wise, London, January 1937, Córdoba
Clifford Wolstencroft, Oldham, March 1938, Aragon
Thomas Woods, Dublin, December 1936, Córdoba

Anthony Yates, Glasgow, February 1937, Jarama
Stephen Yates, London, November 1936, Madrid
W.J. Young, Sydney, Australia, July 1938, Ebro

Francisco or Frank Zamora, Abercrave, South Wales, January 1938, Teruel

Index

Note: page numbers in bold refer to illustrations.